CIRCULAR
MOTION

Copyright © 2007 David Ashe

Published by dash Media Networks

Book Design by dash Media Arts

Cataloging in Publication Data is on file with the Library of Congress.

ISBN# 978-0-6151-5021-5

www.circularmotion.net

PRINTED IN THE UNITED STATES OF AMERICA

CIRCULAR
MOTION

4 SHORT PLAYS
A ONE ACT
AND
A SCREENPLAY

by

David Ashe

Contents

Introduction

Everyone is creative. And each person expresses their creativity in a different way. A farmer who can "create" a crop from the soil is no less creative than any of the great artists that can come to mind. For some creativity is expressed in different ways at different times in their lives.

So many of us with great intention take pen in hand, or put hands to keyboard and set out to "create". The initial impulse followed by the serious attempt usually gives way to the reality of the daunting task. But, those who persevere feel emboldened by a true sense of accomplishment, regardless of the quality of the work.

Intermittently throughout the 1990's I felt that "urge" to express myself through the written word. So, this is my contribution from that brief period when my creative outlet took the written form and I decided to add my voice to those that believed they could add to humanity's great body of creative work.

WORTH A THOUSAND WORDS

CHARACTERS: Ken, Gail

SCENE ONE

A couple is in a museum looking at piece of art.

KEN: (in disbelief) Are you kidding me? It sucks.... I'm not getting anything at all from this.

GAIL: (calmly) You must be blind.... That's one of the most warm and comforting pieces I've ever seen in my life.... It reminds me of home... Being with my family. (wistful sigh)

KEN: I don't get it.

GAIL: That's because you're a man... You have no feeling or emotion.

KEN: Hey what're you talking about? I was voted sensitive guy of the year in 1989.

GAIL: (teasing) Well you've lost your touch.

KEN: You know if this were a woman she'd be a cold fish.

GAIL: What's that supposed to mean?

KEN: Plain, bland.... A real C average.

GAIL: That shows how little you know about women. You can't feel the depth and the character can you?

KEN: (mock anger) Are you calling me shallow?

GAIL: Of course not... Do the words cold fish mean anything to you? (laughing)

KEN: (also laughing) Ouch... Boy does my male ego hurt.

GAIL: Like I said you don't understand women.

KEN: Can you please give me a definitive explanation of women?

GAIL: (smiles) You're so naive.

SCENE TWO

The same museum and piece of art.

JAMES: What?   This is it?   Are you kidding?

KEN: That's what I said. I came here with Gail and she says it's something very deep. Like somehow there's something here a woman could understand and a man couldn't.

JAMES: This? I don't know.... It's just kind of...there.

KEN: (puzzled) I know. I still don't get it.

They stop to contemplate their ignorance and watch an attractive woman pass by.

JAMES: You know I think I could do it with half the female population. And while I was doing it with one half I'd be wondering what it was like with the other half.

KEN: (looking around) Hey lower your voice. That's really not a very 90's kind of thing to say... There are a lot of women around here.

JAMES: (laughing) Sorry .... You want to know the truth Mr. 90's, men aren't as bad as women say we are and women aren't as holy as they think they are.

KEN: Still it's kind of a cliché.

JAMES: Every cliché started somewhere.

(pause)

KEN: (smiling) Yeah I'll bet all the cave men wanted to sleep with one half of the cave women and wondered what the other half was like too.

Ken and James both have a good laugh over this thought.

SCENE THREE

The same museum and piece of art.

GAIL: Now do you know what I mean.

KELLY: (enthusiastic) Oh yeah. It's fantastic. I can really feel it.... I can't believe Ken couldn't get into this. I thought he had more going for him.

They both pause in contemplation.

KELLY:(blushing) You know what this makes me think of... When I was thirteen, and I was at summer camp..... There was a boys camp across the lake that we had activities with....One day I went for a walk with a boy.... I had the biggest crush on him..... Oh what was his name......Paul .....It was a beautiful summer day and we just held hands and walked.... We barely said a thing to each other....Neither one of us knew what to say....(sigh) It was like a dream............(comes out of daydream) I don't think I've felt that comfortable with a member of the opposite sex since then.

GAIL: Yeah.... I keep thinking about the ski trip I took with my family when I was in high school. We stayed in my uncles' cabin. It was just my parents and my sister, but we had such a good time sitting in front of the fire.... We even sang songs. (smiles) It was such fun.

KELLY: (shaking her head) And Ken didn't get it?

GAIL: He said if it were a woman she'd be a cold fish.

KELLY: (still shaking her head) Well.... What can you expect? He's a man.

SCENE FOUR

The same museum and piece of art.

GAIL: Ken what are we doing here?

KEN: Indulge me... Besides I said I was buying lunch. Ok, now what is it about this thing that I'm not getting. Come on.. Give...I want to know what this whole woman's point of view thing is all about.

Ken gives her a legitimately expectant look. As if he really wants to understand.

GAIL: (surprised) You want to know right here and now?

KEN: Yes!

GAIL: (thinking) Um......I....uh....... It's uh.....Well........It's not something you can just explain to someone!

KEN: (exasperated) What do you mean?.....(recovers) Ok..ok. I've been thinking about this..... Ok. Lets see if this makes any sense to you..... It's like when you're young and you fall in love for the first time, and you are high as a kite. I mean it's like you're on drugs. Like what acid must be like. You know what I mean. And you think it's going to last forever and then after you crash real hard you're not willing to go up so high, or at least you're always looking for the ground..... Is it like that.... this whole female thing....? I mean is that the way you see things all the time?

Gail gives Ken a very skeptical look.

KEN: (still reaching) Or.... Is it that you're like that most of the time? Or maybe women are just as jaded as men but men get that way faster and women cover it up better. Come on Gail help me out here I'm trying to figure this thing out...

Ken gives another expectant look. There's an extended pause as they look at each other.

GAIL: (smiling) Ken, this not the kind of thing you can "get"..... You're just going to have to accept us the way we are.......

Ken looks really disappointed.

GAIL: (smugly) Besides no man could understand the brilliance of women.

KEN: (rolls his eyes and smiles) Oh please!! (pause) By the way if you ever tell anyone what I just said I will completely deny the whole thing.

They both laugh as they walk away.

CURTAIN

/1994

FACE TO FACE

CHARACTERS: Jack Franklin and Dr. Syed Ali

SCENE ONE

Jack is sitting in a leather chair in a lawyers office with his head buried in his briefcase. Syed sits at the end of a leather sofa reading a newspaper. There is another man on the sofa between them.

SCENE TWO

Days later Syed is sitting in the same place reading a medical journal.

RECEPTIONIST: (on the phone) Freidman and Klien law offices.

Jack walks into the office and hangs up his coat going over to the receptionist.

JACK: Could you let Mike know that Jack Franklin is here.

Without waiting for a response Jack goes back to the same chair he was sitting in before, opens his briefcase and pulls out a medical journal. He notices that he and Syed are reading the same issue of the same medical journal. As Jack begins to read the magazine, Syed also notices that they are reading the same journal.

SCENE THREE

The next week Syed is standing in front of the receptionist.

RECEPTIONIST: Ok Dr. Ali I see you have your current citizenship papers, but we also need a form that states that your intention is to stay in this country permanently.

SYED: When I talked to Mr. Freidman he said I wouldn't need to bring that in until…

While Syed is talking Jack comes in and goes directly to the receptionist cutting him off in mid-sentence as if he isn't even standing there.

JACK: (hurriedly, looking at his watch) Tell Mike we have a meeting with the AMA board from Washington at three so we don't have time to waste today.

Again without waiting for her to answer Jack turns and heads for the same chair he was sitting in before. Syed and the receptionist stare after Jack for a moment, but he is oblivious to them as he pulls his cellular phone from his briefcase and begins to make a call. Syed continues to look at Jack as the receptionist makes the call.

RECEPTIONIST: (on the phone) Mike, Jack Franklin is here and he says he can't wait.

SCENE FOUR

As Syed walks into the office Jack is sitting in the chair talking on the phone. Syed hangs up his coat, waves to the receptionist and takes his usual seat at the end of the sofa.

JACK: (excited) Marge we're going to be able to double production on the K-1000 and the Flex 806 because of this deal. We'll be able to get to every lab in the country now. (pause) What do mean hire more people? We'll just have to pull double shifts... If I hire more people then how can I give you that raise I promised? (laughing) (pause) A raise and a bonus? Forget it. Your bonus is that you get to work for a great guy like me... Hey what time is my meeting with that guy from the bank? (pause) Ok, I'll be there. Yeah I'll bet he's anxious now that we're going to be rolling in dough. (pause) All right I'll see you when I get back to the office.

Jack is smiling broadly as he kisses the phone before he puts it back in his briefcase. He is obviously very happy and pleased with himself. He stands up, straightens his tie and adjusts his jacket as he almost bounces over to the coffee maker to get some coffee. Syed is still sitting there, and is ignoring Jack. As he sits down with his coffee, Jack can no longer contain himself.

JACK: (to Syed) My friend, I have made the deal of the century.

Syed nods at Jack hoping that will pacify him. It doesn't.

JACK: I am going to make a killing... I'm going to double production on two of my most expensive supplies.

Once again Syed only nods hoping Jack will stop talking. Jack isn't getting the hint.

JACK: You can't believe this set up. The governments' going to pay me to make more money.

Syed now can't help but respond since Jack won't stop.

SYED: That will probably raise the cost of the stillenium nitrate clamp, which will in turn raise the cost of research yet again.

Jack is momentarily startled by Syeds' response, but recovers quickly.

JACK: (almost angry) How do you know so much, what are you a lab assistant or something?

RECEPTIONIST: Dr. Ali, Mr. Freidman will see you now.

Syed gets up to go into back office while Jack is still waiting for an answer.

SYED: (resentful) No, I am Dr. Syed Ali, and if you check you will find that I'm one of your best customers for the stellenium nitrate clamp. Which I'm sure just went up in price.

Before Jack can say a word Syed turns and walks into the back office.

SCENE FIVE

Jack is sitting in the chair digging through his briefcase. Syed comes in and stops short when he sees Jack. He hangs up his coat and takes his usual place on the sofa. When he sits down Jack looks up and recognizes him.

JACK: (gloating smile) Well if it isn't Dr. Syed Ali.

Syed gives Jack a tense look and nods in acknowledgment.

JACK: So we meet at last eh... You know I did check my records. Maybe I should thank you or something. I've made a lot of money off you in the last few months... (smug) And I'm going to make a lot more.

Jack seems to want to provoke Syed in some way as he waits for a response.

SYED: (curtly) How nice for you. I'm sure you're very happy for yourself.

Jack is obviously glad he got a rise out of Syed.

JACK: You bet I am... I never got a chance to tell you how I pulled this thing off. You know the president's health care bill right, well as part of the preventive health maintenance package I got the AMA to lobby for a medical research subsidy. That means the government is going to pay me to provide more supplies to research labs all over the country.... Is that a beautiful deal or what? Oh, and here's the best part, since I'm not a drug manufacturer I won't be subjected to any of the price controls.

Jack sits back in his chair looking very pleased with himself.

SYED: (disgusted) And I suppose that means you'll be raising prices on all your supplies; and the cost of my research.

JACK: Now you're starting to get the picture... All you doctors got it made but you keep whining about rising costs because you know it will eat into your profits.

SYED: Profits? Those costs will have to be passed on to patients so that we can continue to do our work.

JACK: (almost sneering) Like you give a shit about patients. All you you've got on your mind is your damn research grant.

SYED: (controlled anger) I shouldn't expect you to understand the importance of my work. But I wouldn't even be here if it weren't for your "deal of the century".

JACK: What do you mean you wouldn't be here?

SYED: Your government didn't renew its part of the joint grant it had with my country to pay for my research because of your great subsidy. Because of you I had to come to the United States to continue my work. My wife and my children had to leave their home and schools, and our position in the community to come here... There is no order in your country.

Jack takes a moment to consider this.

JACK: Oh I get it. You're just pissed because now you're not some big shot doctor here like you were back in your country. Yeah, now you're just another lab doctor trying to make it on a little research hand out. Well, that's the way business is done pal. Money talks and bullshit walks... Now "my" kid can go to a private school. And no more public golf courses, it's strictly private clubs from now on.

RECEPTIONIST: Dr. Ali, Mr. Freidman is ready to see you now.

Jack sits back in his chair smiling. Although he's under control Syed is obviously not pleased by the exchange that just took place as he gets up and walks into the back office.

SCENE SIX

Jack is sitting in his usual chair talking on his cellular phone when Syed walks. As soon as he sees Jack he rolls his eyes, shakes his head and takes his usual place on the sofa reading a magazine.

JACK: (on the phone) Ok what's my schedule for the rest of the day? (pause) Move the managers meeting to four, I need to look at some reports beforehand, and tell Simmons I want to see him at three so we can go over a few things before... Hold on Marge I've got another call... Hello... Hi Joan hold on a second Marge is on the other line... Marge I have to go my wife's on hold... What's up Joan?

Jack falls completely silent. His face falls noticeably and he slumps down in his chair. He is staring straight ahead as if in disbelief. There is a long pause before he speaks again.

JACK: (mumbling) Yeah, yeah I'm still here... I heard you... I'll see you when I get home.

Jack continues to sit in the same position slowly taking the phone from his ear. He is obviously shaken. Syed noticed what was going on and is now looking at Jack intently to figure out what is going on. After a long pause Syed can't stand it any longer.

SYED: (concerned) What has happened?

JACK: (still mumbling) Timothy Davis died this morning.

Syed's reaction is similar to Jacks. Stunned disbelief. After a moment Syed recovers somewhat.

SYED: Did you get the letters and the phone calls? His mother sent letters and called everyone who had anything to do with his disease. My work was part of the research that was being done.

JACK: Yeah, I did. Did you see the pictures? Oh my god...

SYED: She came down to our lab once. She was begging and pleading for us to save her son's life... There is only so much we can do....

JACK: My son Jonathan is ten, same as Timothy...God I don't know what I'd do if... (long pause) You know it's his first year of little league. You should see him out there...

SYED: My son is eight years old... I'm trying to teach him how to throw a baseball. Every time he try's the ball slips out of his hand and goes behind him.

JACK: (brightens a bit) That used to happen to Jonathan too. Just tell him to squeeze really tight like he was going to make a fist just before he throws.

Jack and Syed sit in silence for just a moment.

RECEPTIONIST: Jack, Mike is ready to see you now.

Jack quickly puts his phone in his briefcase, gets up and starts toward the back office. Before he goes in he stops and turns toward Syed as if he wants to say something. They see each other for that moment and Jack turns and goes into the office without another word.

SCENE SEVEN

Jack is at the coffee maker in office when Syed walks in. Jack turns around from the coffee maker at the same time that Syed turns around from hanging up his coat. They are standing face to face and for a moment there is silence.

JACK: (stiffly) How are those throwing lessons coming along?

CURTAIN

/1993

TWO WAY MIRROR

CHARACTERS: Ed, Frank, Stan

Three homeless men are in an alley. It's late afternoon and they have stopped there for a rest as they were walking down the alley. Frank and Stan are sitting and Ed is shuffling back and forth trying to stay warm. It's fall and the air is cool and crisp.

ED: (sniffing and shuffling) Hey pass me that bottle man... It's really starting to get cold now.

FRANK: (always gruff) My back always gets stiff as a board this time of year... Feels like a steel pipe is stuck in my spine.

ED: (suddenly excited) Hey man did you hear about that guy who met those aliens...? He had this mark on his neck. It didn't look like no human mark either. Now he says he's one of them. Like he's completely different.......(wistfully) I wonder if I could be one man.... Dude sometimes; I don't know...

STAN: (always vague and faraway looking and sounding) Aliens? Every woman on earth is an alien. They were sent here to destroy men.

FRANK: Every day it's the same thing with you. One bad apple does not spoil the whole barrel.

ED: No man I'm serious... I really feel like an alien sometimes.

STAN: It's true Frank you just can't see the truth can you?   Bottle?

FRANK: Can't see the truth? Ever since my back gave out lifting that pipe I been feeling the truth, much less seeing it... Shit, I went to the doc and he said I got the spine of an eighty year old man....Can't see the truth.. (shaking his head)

ED: You know the first time was when my pops left. I didn't know what was going on.... He just kind of disappeared... Dude, I felt like I was from a different planet kinda ever since... I been an alien since I was twelve years old.

STAN: What about your mother? You still had her. That's all most kids get nowadays.

ED: She died when I was five, so when pops left that was it man. No brothers no sisters no family no nothing.

STAN : (with sudden anger) That's just like a woman to leave you high and dry and on your own. If anything happens to my kid I'll kill that bitch.... (calmer) She didn't have to take my son away just so she could "find" herself....You shouldn't take a boy away from his father like that.... She kept saying things had to change. I never thought she'd really do it. After twenty years together....We came out from Nebraska just a couple of kids....And the best she can do is a note on the kitchen table.... She had a roof over her head, food to eat, clothes to wear.

What the hell did she want from me? Things weren't that bad.... Were they?

FRANK: (unsympathetic) Hey, pass that medicine bottle over here.... You've still got your health, what do you want.

ED: Growing up with no parents can suck sometimes I guess... At first I went from place to place.... Foster homes and shit like that, but I kept on running away. I was better off on my own.... I'm free.... Being on the streets isn't so bad. Man you can do anything you want. It's like you're invisible. You just gotta watch out for cops sometimes.

STAN: There's no way I'm going to let my kid wind up like this... No way on earth. I don't care what I have to do.... Nobody should ever live like this.

There's an extended pause as they seem to contemplate how they are living their lives.

STAN: Why don't you do something about your back?

FRANK: (takes his time answering) In construction, if you're not officially on the payroll you don't get health insurance. They don't care if you're hurt they just want the work to get done. If you can't do the work they just let you go.

ED: Dude, that sucks.

FRANK: After I hurt my back they didn't even know who I was anymore.... They couldn't even see me.... (extended pause) Like when you ask someone on the street for some change so you can get something to eat..... The ones that give you something... it's like they're paying you off so they don't have to see what could happen to them..... And the one's that don't can't even see you at all.... They don't even know you exist....I hear 'em talking sometimes about some guy they saw talking to himself.... Hell if they barely see that guy how're they going to see who he's talking to.... If some guy is talking you can bet your ass he sees someone there... Even if no one else can.

Frank struggles to his feet, obviously wincing at the pain in his back.

FRANK: (reaching for the bottle) That's why we drink our medicine. (takes a drink) The reflections.... are hard on your eyes.

ED: (oblivious to Frank's point) Hey man it's going to get dark soon....let's go over to the park... Maybe we can see some UFO's.

CURTAIN

/1994

DESTINY

CHARACTERS: Abe, Tom, Josh

SCENE ONE

A detective is waiting in the interrogation room of a police department as his partner brings a handcuffed man into the room and sits him down at the table.

TOM: (half joking) Is this our latest postal worker?... How many of these guys can go bananas in one week?

JOSH: Nope. This guy's got a good old fashioned God complex. Thinks he should decide who's going to live and die.

TOM: How many?

JOSH: Seven, as far as we know. A couple of junkies, a few hookers, and a husband and wife in their BMW.

TOM: (finally turns to ABE) Like to spread it around eh buddy? Ok, let's have it, what's your deal what's going on here?

ABE: (serious but not solemn) I had to save them.

TOM: (derisive laughter) You had to save them? Well you didn't do a very good job pal. They're dead. (turns serious) Now what the fuck is going on here?

ABE: (sighs) It's a long story.

TOM: (sitting down) Guess what, you're not going anywhere for a long time. Pull up a chair Josh the man is going to tell us a story.

ABE: (calmly) I had to save them from themselves. The way they were living their lives they could never be in alignment with the universe.

TOM: What the fuck?

ABE: Their spirits' could never be at one with the universal spirit if they continued to live the way they were living. And it only would have gotten worse if they continued on the course they were taking. I allowed them to release their present bodies and let their spirits start over again.

JOSH: So this was some kind of religious thing?

ABE: This is more than that. Religion is only a means to an end. The purpose of all religions is the same. To bring man as close to the universal spirit as possible. The problem is that most people can't get past the words to get to the meaning. That there's one universal spirit and the illusion of separation is the inherent flaw within all of humanity.

TOM: (shaking his head) I can see it now, the papers are going to be calling this guy the New Age murderer.

ABE: This has nothing to do with any age, new old or other-wise. It's always been this way, it's just that now more people are beginning to see the light. These kinds of ideas have been around for years. Jung is famous for bringing the collective unconscious to modern psychology. And today physicists are starting to prove what has always been true.

JOSH: (curious) What's always been true?

ABE: That separation is an illusion. Because of man's inherent flaw we have set up a completely false way of life. Time doesn't exist. Past, present and future are just words with no meaning. The concept of time as we know it is man made. We use time to separate events, one from another. Every event affects another. Everything in the universe is interrelated. Both of your lives will be changed just because you've come in contact with me.

TOM: Don't bet on it pal.

ABE: I don't have to bet on it because I know it. The separation among humans is only a negative projection of our inherent flaw. Race, religion, sex and everything else. These differences only exist because collectively we choose to see them. Now more and more people are starting to wake up and see that there really are no differences. It's like having a greater depth of field like on the lens of a camera. Even though we are the ones who set this whole ridiculous thing up, we can still get past it.

TOM: Look who's talking about ridiculous?

JOSH: (interested) What's this inherent flaw of humanity that you keep talking about?

ABE: Like I said before it comes back to separation. The flaw is that humans have a choice of whether or not to live in accordance with the universe. You never see a flower deciding whether or not to open when the sun comes out. Plants don't decide what they want to be when they grow up. You see man, in our infinite ignorance, got it completely wrong back when we were figuring out the order of the earth. We thought we were on top, but the truth is we're on the bottom. Everything we believe is upside down and backwards. Plants, vegetation is actually the purest spiritual entity. Their entire existence is in complete alignment with its purpose and there is no variance from that purpose, ever. They also make no sound. The communication they have with the universe is one of a pure exchange of energy.

TOM: (sarcastically) So you think plants should rule the world eh? (rolls his eyes)

ABE: No, what I'm talking about is the spiritual order of the earth.

JOSH: So animals must come next then right?

ABE: Exactly, they also come into their existence at one with their purpose. They do what they do out of pure instinct. Because they make sound they have the ability to communicate so they have their own illusions of separation and scarcity. Their basic need to conquer the other to sustain their own survival is similar to our own. Although on a primitive and honest level. Humans never want to admit to it.

TOM: Now he's Dr. Doolittle. He talks to the animals.

JOSH: That means we're last then because we can talk.

ABE: Well that's one reason. Human beings use verbal language for deception more than anything else. Most often when anyone speaks they're not telling the truth. Not even the truth as they believe it to be. Real communication doesn't need words. Even when people communicate with language they do so not because of the words, but because of the real meaning and feeling and energy that the words evoke. And language has nothing to do with ones purpose on the planet that's for sure.

TOM: Well I'll tell you what buddy, my purpose is to put nut cases like you behind bars.

ABE: Maybe that is your purpose. If so it's only because of the inherent flaw in humanity. And it's a noble pursuit because you're trying to help the human condition, if you perform your purpose well and with compassion...But what if that's not your purpose. Perhaps the masks that you wear won't allow you to find your true purpose. Your passion, the thing that resonates in your core being. Did someone tell you this was the only way you could serve humanity? Language is only the most common mask people use. The people who are in the most pain, the ones that are very very far away from their own spiritual flame wear much heavier masks. The lost souls who use destructive chemicals to replace their spirit, or those who use physical desires as a way to deceive themselves rather than a real communication of feeling and energy. Or even those who use power and money to further the illusion of separation for their own gain.

TOM: So you are a religious fundamentalist wacko!

ABE: I told you this is bigger than religion. This is about the universal spirit.

TOM: Yeah, call it what you want, but it sounds to me like you're saying that God told you to kill those people. Well it won't wash with me pal. You can try that insanity defense but it won't work. I think you're nuts but the DA will rip you to shreds. You did read him his rights didn't you Josh.....Josh snap out of it!

JOSH: (comes out of a daze) What? Uh, yeah I read him his rights. Everything went by the book.

TOM: Well get him out of here, story time's over.

JOSH: You said you were trying to save them by letting their spirits come back again and start over?

ABE: Yes, people in that much pain who are so far away from realizing the universal spirit in themselves and the world would live on in confusion and pain and probably hurt others in the process of maintaining their despair.

JOSH: Yeah but what if you're wrong? What if they had hit bottom and were about to get help. What if in five years or ten they turned everything around and wound up making a difference in someone else's life. Now we'll never know.

ABE: They needed my help. It was my purpose.

TOM: (sharply) Josh! Get his ass out of here. We've got work to do.

CURTAIN

/1994

CIRCULAR MOTION
(ONE ACT)

SCENE ONE

Karen and Teri are sitting in a bustling bar dressed in business attire.

TERI

(anxious)

So what did he say?

KAREN

(in a masculine type voice)

'We're not going to be doing anything like that around here'.
(angrily) Can you believe that. And then he started working on
something on his desk. Like I was dismissed or something.

TERI

You mean you asked him to be more courteous and all he could say was we're not going to be doing anything like that around here?

KAREN

Those were his exact words.

TERI

What an asshole... Did you give him that stuff about positive reinforcement and increased productivity?

KAREN

I gave him the whole speech.

TERI

What about higher profits and better customer satis...

KAREN

(interrupts but not harshly)

I'm telling you I gave him everything. It was humiliating...

TERI

So what are you going to do?

KAREN

I don't know... The worst part is that now he probably thinks I'm just some weak woman who can't get things done... So much for my future there.

They both pause to sip their drinks and contemplate KAREN's last statement.

TERI

(trying to be encouraging)

It can't be that bad... Who knows maybe he didn't give the whole thing a second thought.... I thought you really liked that job? Weren't you starting to work with the lighting people on sets or something like that?

KAREN

Yeah, but in the last few months I started to feel like I wanted... I don't know... something more than just work. The problem was that I was putting in eighty hours a week. Minimum! I didn't have a life.

TERI

I remember I could never get ahold of you.

KAREN

So I talked to him about reducing my hours. That's when things started to go down hill. Maybe things were always bad and I was just too busy to notice... Anyway I started to be in the office more and look what happened.... Is a little courtesy to much to ask?

TERI

Is that why you started talking about grad school all of sudden? I don't know KAREN, going back school at thirty four... You'd be thirty six or thirty seven by the time you finished and you'd still have to find a job after that.

KAREN

(sarcastically)

Thanks for doing the math for me... It just seems like there ought to be more then this...

                              TERI

                            (grinning)

Oh, come on things aren't that bad. So you had a little set back at
work, big deal.

*KAREN leans back in her chair looking depressed and takes a sip of
her drink.*

                              TERI

Is that a new shade of nail polish. It really looks good on you.

                             KAREN

                          (still gloomy)

Don't try to sell me a good mood. Is that how you deal with
everything?

                              TERI

Hey don't knock sales. It's a great way to earn a living. It's just like
putting on a little show everyday. You get someone in a meeting and
start talking. Next thing you know you're closing them. It's a lot more
fun than you think.

                             KAREN

You make it sound easy, but how do you handle the rejection.

                              TERI

Everyone goes through slumps, that's just part of the game. I learned
that from the guys I work with. They always say keep swinging at
good pitches and you'll always hit your way out.

KAREN

(blank look)

What?

TERI

(rolls her eyes)

It means don't give up.

KAREN

I don't know... I still think grad school is worth a try. At least it's a place to start.

TERI

All that studying? Four years was enough for me.

A waitress enters sets a drink down in front of TERI.

WAITRESS

This is from the gentleman over there (pointing)

KAREN and TERI look off stage. TERI acknowledges the drink.

WAITRESS

He wants to know if he can join you.

TERI

Tell him thanks for the drink but we won't be staying much longer. Maybe some other time.

KAREN and TERI look at each other and laugh.

KAREN

(glancing off stage again)

He didn't look all that bad, maybe you shouldn't have thrown him back so fast.

TERI

Oh come on, you know there are plenty of fish left in the sea any time you want one.

KAREN

That depends on what kind of fish you want. I'd prefer the kind that didn't swim away. You're the one who had to remind me that I'm thirty four.

TERI

I'm only a year younger then you are. Besides, you know relationships don't work anyway.

(looking at her watch)

Uh oh, it's getting late. I have to go. I have a dinner meeting at nine.

SCENE TWO

A tall intense looking man is hunched over a large wooden desk with paper all over it.

ALAN

(on the phone, slightly angry but not loud)

Thompson what's happening with the Bright Line account?

(pause)

What do you mean you're working on it!? Do I need to remind you that you're supposed to be bringing clients in and I mean signed sealed and delivered? I thought you were a closer.

(pause)

I want an answer by next week, and I mean Friday. No exceptions.

(pause)

Just get it done.

ALAN looks at the phone shaking his head and slams it down in anger.
He then reaches for a videotape on his desk, puts it in the tape
machine next to his desk and turns it on.

ALAN

(still angry as he looks at the tape)

Shit! (yelling) KAREN, get in here!

KAREN comes into the office looking as if she's bracing herself.

ALAN

Have you seen this! It's the wrong fucking tape.

KAREN

What is it? What did they send?

ALAN

I can't believe this. They sent the Hijacked tape instead of the
Thrillkill tape. I talked to that jerk myself too.... What time did this get
here?

KAREN

I think it came some time this morning. I don't know maybe nine...

ALAN

Nine! You mean you let it sit on my desk all day and didn't tell me.

KAREN

(trying to remain calm)

I put it right in front of your chair where you would be sure to see it as soon as you came in.

ALAN

Well why didn't you tell me what it was!?

KAREN

I didn't know what was until right now.

ALAN

What!? You knew that tape was supposed to be coming in today! I've got to have this video copied and shipped by next Wednesday! It's on the schedule!

KAREN

But how...

ALAN

(shouting)

No buts damnit! Get the schedule. I'll show it to you.

KAREN

(stammering)

But...

ALAN

(pointing off stage)

Get it!

KAREN walks off stage looking shaken and angry and returns with the schedule book and hands it to ALAN. She starts to back away.

ALAN

No, stay right there.

ALAN flips through a few pages in the book and drops it on the desk right in front of where KAREN is standing.

ALAN

(pointing in the book)

What does that say?

KAREN

ALAN, I...

ALAN

(interrupting)

What does it say!?

KAREN

(controlled anger)

Drop date for Thrillkill. ALAN I know what it says. I wrote it there.

ALAN

That's right you wrote it so you should know better than to just leave this tape lying around.

KAREN

I didn't leave it lying around I put it...

ALAN

(interrupting)

You could have looked at it yourself. Why didn't you just open it up and look at the tape for yourself. You wrote the schedule you knew what we needed.

KAREN

(stern)

I put the tape on your desk for you to look at. ALAN it's not my fault they sent the wrong tape.

ALAN

Well that's not helping us get the job done, now is it? Just what I need excuses...

(looking at his watch)

All right, it's two thirty. If we get a messenger we can have Thrillkill here by four. Maybe we can get a few hours worth of dubbing in before the end of the day. I want you to call those guys, and tell them what happened so they can get the right tape ready for the messenger. You got that!?

KAREN

(defiantly)

Yes. I have that.

KAREN begins to walk off stage.

ALAN

(as she's leaving)

When you're finished with that, come back in here. I guess we're going to have to go over this schedule again and again until we get it right!

SCENE THREE

KAREN is sitting in the same bar later that evening as TERI walks in and sits next to her at a table. There's an empty glass in front of her and she's waving for a waitress.

TERI

Hey, what's going on?

(looking at the empty glass)

Looks like you started without me.

KAREN

(obviously angry)

That was the first of many.

TERI

What's wrong? You sounded kind of funny when you called.

KAREN

(loudly)

I'm going to kill him... I don't know... I'm just going to kill him!

TERI

What did he do this time?

A waitress finally comes over to KAREN and TERI.

WAITRESS

What can I get for you?

KAREN

Double vodka.

TERI

I'll just have a margarita.

(as the waitress leaves)

What happened? I haven't seen you drink double vodkas' in a long
time.

KAREN

I just feel like I could kill him.

TERI

(looking around)

You really should stop saying that.

KAREN

Some mix-up with a tape. He just went nuts. He was yelling and
screaming and ordering me around like I was a little kid. I didn't have
anything to do with it.

TERI

What set him off? Did something else happen?

KAREN

I don't know... There wasn't anything else going on. I heard him
yelling at someone on the phone as usual, but there wasn't anything...

*The waitress comes back with the drinks. TERI reaches for her purse,
but KAREN puts enough money for both drinks.*

KAREN

I got it. I might as well pay while I still can....I hate that he can get to me like this...I've never been so... I remember once when I was thirteen and my dad caught me going through his closet. He was so mad. He would act just like ALAN when he was mad. Always cutting you off, just yelling and screaming.

TERI

(surprised)

Your dad? He's such a nice guy, at least he's always nice to me.

KAREN

You've never seen him when he's angry. What a nightmare. It takes a lot to get him going, but once he's mad, watch out. It's almost like he's irrational or something. Just like ALAN was today...I couldn't wait to get away to college. But I never thought anyone else could ever make me feel this bad.... I can't believe he blamed me for that... It was just a stupid tape.

KAREN downs the rest of her drink.

TERI

You better slow down there. If you keep that up you might actually do something you'll regret....

(grinning)

I'm not the only one who heard you say you wanted to kill someone.

KAREN gives a half smile.

KAREN

I like your hair. When did you get it cut?

TERI

(running her hand through her hair)

Yesterday. I went to Candy again. She keeps trying to sell me on a perm, but I don't know. I might just let it grow after this... So, what are you going to do?

KAREN

(heavy sigh)

I don't know. I feel like just quitting and never going back.

TERI

You've got to confront him. You can't let him get away with this.

KAREN

I know, I know. But I really don't want to.

(looks at her watch)

I've got to go pretty soon, I'm still going to try and study for the GMAT tonight. Grad school's got to be better than this.

TERI

If you want to take two, or three years out of your life and get heavily into debt it is.

KAREN

Thanks but I don't need another math lesson.

TERI

I still think you should go in there tomorrow and let him have it. Give it back to him, just like he dished it out.

KAREN

I think you're forgetting that he could fire me any time he wants. After today who knows how much longer I'll be around.

They both pause to look around the bar.

TERI

Look at him.

(nods her head in the direction

of a man sitting alone at the bar)

KAREN

(turns her head to look)

That's what I need. Someone to take me away from all this.

TERI

He couldn't hurt.... But what you really need to do is give ALAN a piece of your mind!

KAREN

(finally smiling)

I think I'd rather have him. I knew there was a reason we always came place.

TERI

He'd probably wind up being a jerk. Besides it wouldn't last.

KAREN

Why do you keep saying things never work out? You and Richard have been together for three years.

TERI

Richard and I have an arrangement. Neither one of us is willing to make a commitment. That's why we're able to stay together. Haven't I told this before?

KAREN

Yeah, but I still don't believe you...

(looks at her watch again)

I really have to get going.

TERI

Give 'em hell tomorrow.

KAREN

(rolling her eyes)

We'll see.

SCENE FOUR

ALAN is in his office sitting at his desk doing paperwork. KAREN starts to enter and stops, looking as if she's trying to steel herself for battle.

KAREN

ALAN I...

ALAN

KAREN, come in I want to talk to you.

KAREN

There's something I've got...

ALAN

Later. I want to get this over with. Look. I... Uhm...(heavy sigh, as he begins to fidget with things on his desk and look very uncomfortable) I... Well, I think I may have been just a little hard on you yesterday about that tape... I realize that it may not have been entirely your fault.

KAREN

ALAN...

ALAN

Just hold on and let me finish. I know we talked awhile ago about how things were going and how you felt.... You mentioned something about courtesy or understanding or something like that.... I realize that I may not have been completely responsive then, and... well... Look, I've got to keep this place going. This is "my" business.

ALAN starts to pace back and forth behind KAREN. He's obviously uncomfortable and agitated.

ALAN

I've had a lot on my mind for some time now. I... Well I guess you could say I've been having some personal problems... I... It's just that... Well the thing is that Jill and I are getting a divorce.

(heavy sigh)

It's been coming on for a long time now, and she decided... I mean "we" decided that it would probably be the best thing for both of us. She wanted to go to counseling, but that stuff is just bullshit. Either you can make it or you can't....

KAREN looks shocked and is frozen in her chair.

KAREN

What happened? I mean I always thought...

ALAN

(angrily)

What happened? She's bailing out on me that's what happened. I'm trying to run a business here and all she can talk about is how I'm never around and what kind of life is this and the kids don't even know their own father....

ALAN stops pacing and leans on a television staring off into space.

ALAN

(shaking his head)

Maybe she's right. Maybe I spend too much time working. But what does she want me to do... This place... This place is mine. It's all mine. Nobody tells me what to do. I make all the decisions. And we've done some good work here. She knows that. And she sure never complained about the money I've made. I think I've done pretty well by her. And now this...

KAREN

(sympathetic)

I'm really sorry ALAN. I had no idea you and Jill were having any problems at all. What're you going to do?

ALAN comes over to sit on the edge of his desk right next to KAREN.

ALAN

(weary)

I don't really have a choice. She's leaving one way or another.... You know it's funny, she used to work here. When I first started out I couldn't afford to hire anyone else. She quit her job to help me. She just jumped right in. She made all the difference. I probably wouldn't have all this without her. Well she's getting half now anyway.

ALAN reaches for KAREN and caresses her face. He looks at her with an odd smile that suggests that he's remembering his wife sitting in that chair and not really seeing KAREN.

ALAN

(softly)

I really appreciate you letting me blow off some steam here. I didn't know I was going to get going like this.

KAREN

(very sympathetic)

That's all right. Sometimes you just need someone to...

Before KAREN can finish her sentence ALAN leans over and kisses her.

SCENE FIVE

KAREN and TERI are in the bar.

TERI

(in disbelief)

On the sofa, in his office?

KAREN nods her head. She is beaming.

TERI

When?

KAREN

Yesterday.

TERI

And you waited this long to tell me! Why didn't you call me?

KAREN

I was kind of in shock. I had no idea this was going to happen.

TERI, still with a look of disbelief, takes a long drink and leans back in her chair for a moment.

TERI

Well... How was it?

KAREN
(lowering her voice)

He's not as big as I thought he might be... but it was great, I mean he lasted forever.

TERI

Did you? (raising her eyebrows)

KAREN
(smiling)

Twice!

TERI takes another long sip of her drink, thinking about the situation.

TERI

So when is he getting divorced?

KAREN

I don't know... But he said they definitely decided.

TERI

But technically, he's still married.

KAREN

Well, yes...

(emphatically)

But he's getting a divorce!

TERI

How long was he married?

KAREN

I don't know. Pretty long, I guess.

TERI

How many kids?

KAREN

Two.

TERI

Young?

KAREN

Seven and ten.

TERI sighs heavily and downs the rest of her drink. She stops a waitress passing by.

TERI

Two more of the same.

KAREN

No more for me, thanks.

TERI

Bring both of them anyway.

The waitress walks away and TERI gives KAREN a long look.

KAREN

What!?

TERI

Can't you see what he's doing?

KAREN

What? What're you talking about?

TERI

KAREN!?

(looking as if KAREN should understand)

KAREN

(defensively)

Why can't you just be happy for me? This could be the break I've been waiting for.

TERI

KAREN, I'm your best friend. Of course I want you to be happy. I just don't want to see you get hurt again.

KAREN

(still defensive)

I'm not going to get hurt. And, he's not doing anything... Besides, he needs me.

TERI

Don't you realize that a few days ago you wanted to kill this man?

KAREN

Yeah, but his wife had just left.

TERI

So every time something goes wrong he'll treat you like shit?

KAREN

No! Getting a divorce is not just some little thing.

The waitress returns with the drinks.

WAITRESS

That'll be six fifty.

TERI lays the money on the tray.

TERI

Thanks.

TERI takes a long sip of her drink.

TERI

You know what's going to happen don't you? Five, ten years down the road you'll be in the same spot as his soon-to-be ex-wife.

KAREN

No I won't. Because I work there every day and we'll be together all the time. I'll really be involved in his life.

TERI

She used to work there too.

KAREN

It'll just be different this time.... TERI, he needs me.

TERI

What about what you need? Remember Jason. He was perfect for you.

KAREN

He was... too right. Sort of, too perfect. I don't know. It probably would have gotten boring.

TERI

(sarcastically)

So for excitement you want a guy who just found out he's getting divorced?

KAREN

You just don't understand.

TERI

What about when you were with Jack. Don't you remember what that was like? Even after you found out he was married, it still took you six months to stop seeing him.

KAREN

He lied to me! And this situation is completely different. I know all I need to know about ALAN. I can make this work.

TERI sits back in her chair as if she's defeated. Shaking her head she sips from her drink.

TERI

Grad school would be better than this.

KAREN

Didn't you tell me that grad school was for people who wanted to avoid living their lives?

TERI

(emphatically)

Just think about it.

SCENE SIX

KAREN enters ALAN's office carrying some files. As she walks in he and Cindy, an office assistant who is younger and more attractive than KAREN, are standing very close together; as if they had just been kissing. They both suddenly look up and move away from each other as soon as KAREN walks in. Cindy, starts to walk out.

ALAN

Make sure that tape gets to the dub house on time, Cindy.

KAREN has a look of shock and disbelief on her face. She stops to watch Cindy leave as she passes by.

CINDY
(smiling)

Hi KAREN.

KAREN is drained and speechless. When KAREN turns to look at ALAN he is still watching Cindy as she walks away. KAREN's eyes meet ALAN's. ALAN breaks their extended gaze and sits at his desk.

ALAN

What is it KAREN? What do you want?

KAREN slowly slumps down into the chair in front of ALAN's desk still holding the files.

KAREN
(in shock, she is shaken and stammering)

I... I... I quit.... I just wanted to... to tell you... that I quit and... I'm going back to school.

ALAN

What are you talking about? The last thing you need to do is waste your time in some MBA program. They have no idea what it's like in the real world. If they did they wouldn't have time to...

KAREN

(still in shock)

I can't believe this.

ALAN

I know what you're thinking, but...

KAREN

(very emotional)

You're just like him!

ALAN

Who? Look KAREN I've got work...

KAREN bursts into tears. ALAN is visibly taken aback.

ALAN

(hesitant)

Who am I like? What are you talking about?

KAREN tries to control herself after realizing what ALAN has asked her.

ALAN

What's your problem?

KAREN

(still trying to not to cry)

NOTHING!

ALAN

(exasperated)

Just tell me what happened.

KAREN

NOTHING HAPPENED!

KAREN begins sobbing again.

ALAN

Look, KAREN, if this is about Cindy I...

KAREN

SHUT UP, ALAN!

ALAN

I...

KAREN breaks down again. She buries her head in her hands. ALAN watches, then goes around the desk and puts his hand on KAREN's shoulder. KAREN doesn't seem to notice until ALAN leans in to kiss her. At first she responds to him, then startled, she jumps out of the chair and slaps ALAN's face. KAREN slowly begins to back away from ALAN, still clutching the files.

KAREN

I have to go... I... I can't do this.... I quit... I have to... get out of here.

SCENE SEVEN

KAREN is sitting at a table in the usual bar looking very collegiate (khaki pants, navy crew sweater, penny loafers). TERI hurries in.

KAREN

Hi. I got you a margarita.

TERI

(hugging KAREN then sitting next to her)

Thanks. It's good to see you again. It looks like grad school agrees with you.

KAREN

Are you kidding? I'm exhausted. This is the first break I've had in months... Are those new diamond earrings?

TERI

I finally dragged Richard to that jewelry store we used to go to. I told him we weren't leaving without them.

KAREN

Is he ever going to pop the question?

TERI

I wouldn't let him if he tried. Why ruin a good thing? But, what about you? How's school going?

KAREN

Pretty good. I mean it's a lot of work and all, but I really feel like I'm learning something useful... It's just that...

(lowering her voice)

I don't know, I think something's going on with one of my professors.

TERI

What do you mean?

KAREN

(distressed)

Well, it seems like he's always picking on me in class. He calls on me all the time and any time I don't know the answer he makes some kind of comment. And he doesn't do that to anyone else. At first I thought he just didn't like me, but it seems like he's always looking at me. And when I talked to him after class one time... it really felt like he was coming on to me.

TERI

(look of concern)

Really? What're you going to do?

KAREN

(heavy sigh)

I don't know... He is kind of cute, but... just before I left, he said he wanted to see me when I got back... in his office.

CURTAIN

/1996

BEHIND THE SHADES

(SCREENPLAY)

FADE IN:

INT: SHARON'S BEDROOM-MORNING

The bedroom is that of a single woman. It's very neat and modern. SHARON is attractive, intelligent, and in her early thirties. It's early Monday morning. The silence in the room is broken by the telephone ringing.

>   SHARON
>   (groggy)
>   Hello.

We hear her mother through the receiver.

>   MOTHER
>   Hi Sharon. Did I wake you?
>   You should be up by now
>   anyway.

> SHARON
> Hi mother. I was just about
> to get up.

Sharon's alarm goes off just as she says this.

> MOTHER
> What happened with that man
> you told me about
> yesterday? What was his
> name? You sounded so
> strange when I talked to
> you.

> SHARON
> (heavy sigh)

> You don't want to know.
> I've got to get ready for
> work. I'll call you this
> afternoon and tell you the
> whole story. You won't
> believe what happened to me
> this weekend. I've got to
> go, I'll talk to you later.

CREDITS ROLL OVER:

Sharon is getting ready for work. As she leaves
her apartment the credits end.

> DISSOLVE TO:

EXT. SMALL MODERN OFFICE BUILDING

CUT TO:

INT. STAFF ROOM OF "MODERN L.A. MAGAZINE"

Sharon works at "Modern L.A. Magazine as a
reporter. The staff room is very busy. Someone
at every desk is either on the phone or
working on their computer terminal. Sharon
hurries in late and flustered. She heads
straight for her desk.

> MALE VOICE OFF SCREEN
> So nice of you to join us.

                    SHARON
                (sarcastically)

Are you kidding, this
magazine could run itself.
Didn't you know that
everyone in this town has a
story to tell?

When she gets to her desk she immediately
reaches for the phone.

                    SHARON
                (distraught)

Patti. You would not
believe the weekend I had.
Hold on.

        (Answers another line)

Sharon Phillips.

                (pause)

Yes Frank, the Kasten story
will be in on time. Will
you relax? I got my degree
in journalism remember?

            (back to Patti)

Patti? Are you free for
lunch? I'll tell you all
about it then.

                (pause)

I can't talk about it right
now, my editor's breathing
down my neck.

                (pause)

Give you a hint? Patti this
is my life not a cheap
novel.

                (pause)

Yes it involves a man... Now
that I thing about it could
be a cheap novel. But, I've

                    got to go. Twelve thirty
                    ok? How about Kristy's?
                    Fine I'll see you then.

After she puts the phone down Sharon stares off
into space and shakes her head, as if in
disbelief.

CUT TO:

EXT. RESTAURANT-TRENDY WITH LOTS OF NEON

CUT TO:

INT. RESTAURANT

The restaurant is very trendy, with lofts of
chrome and glass, and neon art on the walls.
Sharon walks toward the hostess and then sees
PATTI. PATTI, a beautiful model in her mid-
twenties, is at a table in the middle of the
restaurant.

                         SHARON
                  Hi. Sorry I'm late.

                          PATTI
         (before Sharon can settle into her seat)

                    Well!? Well!? Come on
                    Sharon you got me really
                    curious on the phone this
                    morning. Tell me everything
                    that happened in detail.
                    You sounded really weird on
                    the phone.

                         SHARON
                    I guess you can tell I'm
                    losing it. You should love
                    this since you specialize
                    in twisted relationships. I
                    can't believe this happened
                    to me. I'm fairly normal
                    when it comes to dealing
                    with men.

PATTI
(anxious)

Would you quit stalling and
tell me what happened!

SHARON
Basically, I met a guy, I
fell in love and then
disaster.

PATTI
Sharon, I need details.
Give me details!

SHARON
Ok. Ok.

DISSOVLE TO:

EXT. EXPENSIVE DEPARTMENT STORE

CUT TO:

INT. DEPARTMENT STORE-AFTERNOON

Sharon is in the lingerie department of a very
upscale department store, looking at different
items. Picking them up and holding them up to
her body, and putting them down.

SHARON (VO)
(to Patti)

Well I was in Robinson's
Friday afternoon. It seemed
like an ordinary day in the
mall, and I wound up in the
lingerie department. I must
have been daydreaming or
fantasizing or something
while I was looking around,
because when I looked up
there was this guy kind of
staring at me. Or at least
I thought he was. Anyway,
he seemed to be looking for
something at first, but

somehow we started looking
at each other and flirting.

Sharon holds a very skimpy frilly bustier up.
KURT, a very attractive man in his mid-
thirties, approaches Sharon unnoticed.

                    KURT
That would look perfect on
you.

                    SHARON
What..?? Who me? Do you
mean me?

                    KURT
Of course I mean you. Go
try it on and let me take a
look.

                    SHARON
              (laughing)

Thanks but I'll take your
word for it.

                    KURT
Hi. My name is Kurt. If
you'd like my opinion on
any of your other lingerie
selections please feel free
to ask.

                    SHARON
Well Kurt, are you some
kind of expert in women's
lingerie?

                    KURT
No. But I'm an interested
amateur. And I'm always
willing to learn. Miss…
Mrs…?

                    SHARON
Miss. Phillips. Sharon
Phillips.

                    KURT
        Right. As I was saying
        Sharon anything you'd like
        to teach me, I'd be willing
        to learn. In fact, I think
        we should continue this
        discussion over dinner. How
        about it?

                 SHARON (VO)
        I must have been crazy to
        let a guy in women's
        lingerie pick me up, but he
        was cute and I just
        couldn't resist.

                    SHARON
        Well…

                 (pause)

        Ok.

Sharon is still holding the bustier.

                    KURT
        Let me take care of that
        for you.

                    SHARON
                 (embarrassed)

        Oh no. I couldn't let you
        buy this for me.

                    KURT
        I insist. Like I said, it's
        perfect for you.

Before Sharon can protest any further he takes
the bustier to the sales counter. Sharon
follows closely behind.

                    SHARON
        You really don't have to do
        this. I mean, we don't even
        know each other. Really you
        don't…

> KURT
>
> Don't worry we'll get to
> know each other. Tell you
> what, if you don't like it
> you can give it back to me.
> But I know you'll love it.
> Trust me.

Kurt pays for the item with a platinum American
Express car. Sharon is obviously impressed.

CUT TO:

INT. SHARON'S LIVING ROOM-EVENING

Sharon's apartment is neat and clean. It is
obviously well thought out with matching
colors for the sofa, pillows, rugs, and drapes.
It has the usual electronic equipment and is
modern without being trendy.

> SHARON
>
> Make yourself at home. I'm
> just going to take a quick
> shower and change. I have
> some wine in the
> refrigerator if you'd like
> some.

We see Kurt pouring himself some wine, looking
around the apartment, and turning on the TV.

CUT TO:

INT. BATHROOM

Sharon is in the shower. As she comes out Kurt
is standing in the bathroom with her towel.

> SHARON
> (jumps with fright)
>
> What the..?
>
> (startled)
>
> Whoa! I think you got the
> wrong idea.

                    KURT
                 (advancing)

Oh, I have the right idea.

                    SHARON
                  (firmly)

No Kurt. It's too soon. We
don't even know each other.

There is a long pause as Kurt sizes up the
situation.

                    KURT
                 (apologetic)

My mistake. I guess I got
my signals crossed. We're
still good for dinner
right? Let me make it up to
you.

                    SHARON
                 (softening)

Well… Ok. But let's take it
slow.

Kurt returns to the living room and Sharon gets
dressed for dinner. As Sharon is entering the
living room she sees Kurt on the phone and
hears him mention someone's name.

                    KURT
                 (hurriedly)

I've got to go Kim. I'll
talk to you later.

                    SHARON
                (suspiciously)

Who was on the phone?

                    KURT
Just a friend.

CUT TO:

EXT. EXPENSIVE RESTAURANT

CUT TO:

INT. RESTAURANT

The restaurant is French, and very elegant.
Sharon and Kurt are seated at a romantic table
for two. They are in the middle of their
conversation as the scene begins.

                    KURT
          Being a reporter must be
          very exciting. Rushing
          around interviewing people
          for late breaking stories
          and all that.

                    SHARON
          Well it's not all that
          exciting. I mean I don't
          really do Woodward and
          Bernstein type reporting.
          But some of the stories I
          do turn out to be kind of
          interesting some times. As
          a matter of fact I'm doing
          a story right now that's
          really getting good. I
          started out doing this
          story on Dennis Kasten, a
          wealthy philanthropist,
          just as a light public
          interest story. On the
          surface this guy looks
          squeaky clean. But this guy
          is really a sleaze. I found
          out that he's been with
          teenage prostitutes. Two at
          a time on some occasions. I
          really found out by
          accident. I was supposed to
          meet him for an interview
          and I was late. Anyway, he
          was pulling away as I was
          driving up, so figured I'd

follow him home and do the
interview there. That's
when I first saw him pick
up a teenage prostitute.

(pause)

I'm sorry I must be
rambling on and on.
Sometimes I get so wrapped
up in my work...

                 KURT
No. Go ahead. It sounds
like a great story. Please,
finish.

                 SHARON
Well, there isn't much more
to it yet. But I'm still
digging.

                 KURT
And you said being a
reporter wasn't exciting.

                 SHARON
Well, sometimes it is. I
guess I just got lucky with
this one... So what do you
do? Anything exciting?

                 KURT
Nothing compared to being a
reporter. I buy things, I
sell things, investments,
real estate, that kind of
thing. You know boring
stuff like that. All I
really do is make money.

                 SHARON
You must be very good at
it.

                    KURT
          I can't complain. But
          enough about me. Tell me
          more about the stories
          you've covered.

                    SHARON
                    (surprised)

          You really want to hear
          more about my work?

                    KURT
          I'm in the palm of your
          hand.

                    SHARON
                    (pause)

          Well, there was one story
          about a dangerous pesticide
          that I covered...

The music comes up as she begins to tell the
story. Sharon's eyes are shining as she enjoys
the attention.

CUT TO:

EXT. PARKING LOT OF RESTAURANT-NIGHT

Sharon and Kurt are standing next to Kurt's
Porsche. There is the usual tension that occurs
at this point in a first date as Kurt and
Sharon decide what to do next.

                    KURT
          Well...

                    SHARON
          Well...

                    KURT
          So... What do you want to do
          now?

                    SHARON
          I don't know...

                         KURT
              Ok... I have a suggestion.

                      (pause)

              Why don't we go back to
              your place have a drink,
              put our feet up and relax?

                       SHARON
                      (relieved)

              That sounds like a
              wonderful idea.

Kurt opens the door for Sharon with a grand
gesture. As he walks around the car Kurt look
very confident and pleased with himself.

INT. KURT'S PORSCHE

Kurt and Sharon ride in silence for a few
minutes. The radio is playing soft music in the
background.

                         KURT
              You know I'm really glad
              you agreed to go out with
              me.

                       SHARON
              Me too... I never would have
              guessed that I'd meet
              someone while I was
              shopping for lingerie.

                         KURT
                      (laughing)

              Believe me I didn't expect
              it to happen either, but I
              just couldn't resist once I
              saw you.

Kurt takes Sharon's hand and kisses it. Kurt
and Sharon continue to hold hands and are
silent. A news flash comes on the radio and
draws their attention.

                    RADIO ANNOUNCER
Our top story this evening,
a well know philanthropist,
Dennis Kasten has been
arrested for solicitation
of prostitution. Mr.
Kasten, a respected
community leader, was
picked up at a
approximately seven thirty
after he allegedly
approached two undercover
police officers. Mr.
Kasten's only comment was
that he stopped to ask the
women how much a newspaper
cost at a nearby newsstand.
All other questions
concerning his arrest will
be handled by his
attorneys.

Kurt and Sharon look at each other and then
burst out laughing.

                    KURT
            (still chuckling)

Well, I guess they blew the
lid off of your story.

                    SHARON
            (smiling)

Yes, but I still have all
the details.

CUT TO:

INT. SHARON'S APPARTMEN LIVING ROOM-SAME NIGHT

As the scene opens we see Kurt dimming the
lights, pouring the wine, a d putting on soft
music.

                    KURT
I know this all seems kind
of corny, but what can I
say, I'm a romantic.

                    SHARON
I think it's sweet.

                    KURT
You know I really want to
thank you. I've really had
a great time just being
with you tonight. No
pressure to put on a show
or do all that posturing
or... I don't know whatever
you call it. But, it's just
easy with you. I don't feel
like I have to impress you,
even though I want to... You
know what I mean.

                    SHARON
I feel the same way.

                    KURT
                 (laughing)

Could it be fate? Kismet?

Kurt gives her a long look then leans in for a
passionate kiss. He then takes her hand and
starts for the bedroom. She hesitates.

                    SHARON
I don't know Kurt. Maybe
it's too soon.

                    KURT
Sharon you know it's right.
When two people feel the
way we do... This is a
special night in our lives.

                    (pause)
          We only have moments in
          this life. Let's make this
          our first moment.

Once again Kurt start toward the bedroom and
this time Sharon follows, dreamy-eyed.

CUT TO:

INT. SHARON'S BEDROOM

Sharon and Kurt enter the bedroom and Kurt
closes the door behind them. Sharon reaches for
the light switch but Kurt stops her. The blue
colored light of the moon shines in through the
shades as pulsating music begins to play. Kurt
roughly gives Sharon a long, deep, passionate
kiss. Sharon responds and they begin to undress
each other frantically. We then see their two
bodies intertwined on the bed, silhouettes. We
can hear their heavy breathing and their moans
of pleasure over the music, which has been
building as the scene fades out on their
intense lovemaking. The next scene shows them
lying together peacefully asleep with the
moonlight shining in on them through the
shades.

                    SHARON (VO)
          He even let me finish
          first.

CUT TO:

INT. LUNCH RESTAURANT

The scene is back to Sharon and Patti at lunch.

                    PATTI
          I can't believe you fell
          for all that crap.

                    SHARON
          I know. But he sounded so
          sincere, and the lights
          were low, the music was
          soft, and the wine was

starting to kick in.
Besides, I tried to resist.

                    PATTI
                (heavy sigh)

Yeah. I know. I would have
done the same thing. Why do
we always fall for it.

                    SHARON
I don't know. Maybe because
we want to believe it so
badly that we just can't
help ourselves.

They both pause to contemplate this fact.

                    SHARON
He might have really meant
what he said.

Patti gives her sarcastic look.

                    SHARON
                (defensively)

Hey I really fell hard for
Kurt.

            (lowers her voice)

He's really great in bed. I
mean he does it… we did it…
Let's just say when we were
together it really did feel
right. Besides, he's got a
convertible Porsche and a
platinum American Express
card. And when we talked,
we talked about me. He was
interested in my career and
how I felt about things.

                    PATTI
                 (sceptical)

Really? Well what about
Lowell? Remember your so-
called boyfriend.

                    SHARON
I don't know. I like
Lowell. I really do. But I
don't know if I love him or
not.

                    PATTI
Well are you in love with
Kurt?

                    SHARON
I don't know… When I'm with
Kurt I feel beautiful and
exciting. He's so cute and
he has a way of being
classy without trying. With
Lowell I just feel plain.
Lowell is like a loafer
that's broken in just the
way it should be; sturdy,
dependable, but plain.

                    PATTI
Sharon, you're comparing
the man to a shoe.

                    SHARON
I know it's terrible. But
you know what I mean. It's
just different with Kurt.

                    PATTI
So what happened next? I
heard what he did right,
now get to the juicy stuff.

                    SHARON
You sound so eager to hear
my misery.

> PATTI
> Sharon, you know it happens
> to all of us. It's what I
> call the other curse. Men.
> Besides, you've heard some
> of my stories.

> SHARON
> That's true. At least try
> and look sympathetic.

> PATTI
> Ok. Ok.
>
> (she gives a sad look)
>
> Now what happened?

CUT TO:

INT. SHARON'S BEDROOM-NIGHT

Sharon and Kurt are in each others arms and we
see them lying peacefully together as the
moonlight shines in through the shades.

> SHARON (VO)
> Well, like I said Friday
> night was beautiful. And
> the next day he turned into
> a different person.

CUT TO:

INT. SHARON'S LIVING ROOM-SATURDAY

Kurt is sitting in the middle of the sofa. He's
wearing only his pants from the previous
evening. He's smoking, eating a sandwich, and
drinking beer. The television is blaring a
football game and Kurt has his feet on the
coffee table. Sharon comes out of the bedroom
and goes directly to Kurt, putting her arms
around his neck.

> SHARON
> Good morning honey. Oh I
> guess I should say good
> afternoon.

Sharon kisses Kurt on the cheek playfully.

                    KURT
                  (stiffly)

        Morning.

Kurt doesn't return her embrace. She then sits
on the sofa next to Kurt and tries to snuggle
up to his shoulder. He doesn't move.

                   SHARON
        What are we watching?

Kurt takes a long drag o his cigarette.

                    KURT
                  (flatly)

        Virginia and Maryland.

                   SHARON
        Oh...

                    KURT
                  (annoyed)

        Could you get me another
        beer?

Sharon looks at Kurt strangely. Kurt ignores
the look and takes another long drag on his
cigarette. Sharon goes into the kitchen and
gets the beer and hands it to Kurt, who takes
it without a word. His eyes barely leave the TV
screen. Sharon stands there in disbelief for a
second and then stalks into the bedroom in
frustration.

CUT TO:

INT. SHARON'S BEDROOM-SATURDAY AFTERNOON

Sharon stalks into the room and plops down on
the bed angrily, arms folded across her chest.
She notices that the light on her answering
machine is blinking for her phone messages.
Still frustrated she hits the playback button.

> MOTHER
> Hi dear. I just called to
> see how you're doing. Give
> me a call when you get the
> chance.

Sharon reaches for the telephone and begins to
dial her mother's number as the next phone
message starts to play.

> LOWELL
> Hi Sharon, it's Lowell.
> I'll be there at about
> three thirty tomorrow to
> fix you faucet like I said
> I would. I'm bringing my
> tools this time so I
> guarantee success. See you
> later.

Sharon immediately stops dialing and looks at
the clock. It reads three fifteen.

> SHARON
> (whispering to herself)
> Oh my god!

CUT TO:

INT. LIVING ROOM-SATURDAY AFTERNOON

Sharon rushes to the room to say something to
Kurt.

Before she can say anything the doorbell rings.
Sharon takes a step toward the door and then
stops and looks back at Kurt. Again, before she
can say something the doorbell rings. Kurt is
looking at her strangely when the door unlocks
and opens. Lowell enters the room. He sees
Sharon first.

> LOWELL
> Hey why didn't you open the
> door? I've got all my tools
> with me...

Lowell sees Kurt and stops in mid-sentence. The
three of them stare at one another for a moment
before Sharon meekly introduces Kurt and Lowell
to each other.

> SHARON
> Hi Lowell… Uh… Lowell this
> is Kurt. Kurt. Lowell.

> LOWELL
> (pause)

> (awkwardly)

Hello…

Kurt says nothing. He frowns at Lowell and then
turns his attention back to the television.

> LOWELL
> (confused)

Sharon, what's going on
here?

> SHARON
> I was…

> LOWELL
> Who is he? What's going on
> here?

> (pause)

Well I guess that's obvious
right?

Lowell drops his tools and sits down shaking
his head.

> LOWELL
> Sharon… How could you do
> this to me? How could you
> do this to us? I mean… What
> does this mean? Are we
> through? Is this it? Over?
> Finished?

(pause)

You know, it's crazy. It's
always the same thing, you
think you're doing the
right thing and then what
happens? Someone shits all
over you.

                    SHARON
Lowell… Please.

Lowell begins to pace back and forth.

                    LOWELL
No… No, it's true. All my
friends used to tell me,
Lowell you're too good to
them, treat them like dirt
and they're yours for as
long as you want them. Not
me though. Nope. Not me.
I'm too nice. Mr. Nice Guy…
What do I say? No, they're
more than objects to be
used and abused. You can't
just toy with people like
that… I should've listened…
I guess I should've
expected something like
this. Someone always gets
hurt. I guess that's how
you find out who has the
most power in a
relationship. Whoever has
the ability to inflict the
most pain wins.

Kurt gets up from the sofa and heads for
Sharon's bedroom.

                    LOWELL
Where are you going?

                         KURT
                  (without stopping)

            I'm bored.

                        LOWELL
            Great. I'm in pain and he's
            bored.

                        SHARON
            Lowell, take it easy will
            you. I really think you're
            overreacting.

                        LOWELL
                   (sarcastically)

            Oh. Ok. I'm overreacting.

                        SHARON
            I…

An awkward silence falls over them for a
moment. Kurt then reappears from the bedroom,
dressed and heading for the front door.

                         KURT
                  (over his shoulder)

            Be ready at eight. I'll
            pick you up.

Sharon and Lowell stare after him as he goes
out of the door.

DISSOLVE TO:

INT. SHARON'S BEDROOM-SATURDAY EVENING

Sharon is sitting at her dressing table
preparing for her date with Kurt. She's talking
to herself in the mirror.

                        SHARON
            I must be insane. I can't
            believe I'm going out with
            this guy after the way he
            acted this morning… Maybe

he's insane… We both must
be insane.

The doorbell rings. Sharon takes a deep breath
and checks herself in the mirror as the
doorbell rings again.

CUT TO:

INT. LIVING ROOM FRONT DOOR-SATURDAY EVENING

Sharon opens the door and Kurt is standing
there smiling and holding a dozen roses. Sharon
looks for a second and then blushes.

> SHARON
> Oh Kurt. They're beautiful.
>
> (VO to Patti)
>
> At this point I think to
> myself is this guy schizoid
> or what?

CUT TO:

EXT. KURT'S PORSCHE DRIVING ON STREET-NIGHT

CUT TO:

INT. KURT'S PORSCHE

> SHARON
> (shyly)
>
> Kurt what was going on this
> morning? Why were you being
> so mean?
>
> KURT
> Was I being mean? I'm
> sorry. I guess I'm kind of
> a grouch in the morning.
> Anyway, didn't you like the
> roses?
>
> SHARON
> (dreamy)
>
> I love the roses.

(comes out of her daydream)

So who did you go out with
before me? I mean what was
she like and everything?

KURT
What do you mean?

SHARON
You know what I mean. Are
you just coming out of a
really bad relationship
with a horrible person, and
am I some kind of a
transitional relationship
to help you get over it? Or
are you getting over a
messy divorce? Or… you know
what I mean.

KURT
(laughing)

You don't have to worry
about a thing. I don't have
any skeletons in my closet.
So I'm yours for the
taking.

Sharon looks frustrated by his response.

SHARON
Well where are we going?

KURT
(beaming)

You'll see. It's a
surprise. I know you're
going to love this.

Kurt leans over and kisses her on the cheek.

> SHARON
> (VO to Patti)

The whole time I'm thinking
to myself I don't even know
this guy, so why do I think
I'm in love with him.

CUT TO:

EXT. OLD TRADITIONAL LOOKING BAR

CUT TO:

INT. NEW YORK STYLE BAR-SATURDAY NIGHT

The bar is darkly lit with soft jazz playing in
the background. There is long wooden bar with a
brass railing. The booths have tufted leather
and are dark and secluded. The bar is nearly
empty. Lowell is sitting on a barstool all
alone. He has obviously been drinking for a
while and is speaking in the direction of the
bartender who is wiping some glasses.

> LOWELL
> (depressed)

I can't believe it… Over a
year we've been together… I
wonder if she's done this
before. Maybe it would be
better if I didn't know.

> (pause)

She had the nerve to
introduce us! Can you
believe that?

> (pause)

I just can't believe it…

> (to the bartender)

Hey, give me another one.

                          BARTENDER
                         (hesitantly)

Don't you think you've had
enough?

                          LOWELL
                         (sharply)

Yeah, I've had enough
alright. That's why I need
another drink. And this
time make it a triple.

The bartender shrugs and comes over to pour the
drink. While Lowell digs in his pocket for some
money, he notices a woman sitting in a booth by
herself. She's blond, in her early thirties and
very attractive. Lowell takes a long sip from
his drink, then sends the bartender over to her
with a drink.

                          LOWELL
                       (to bartender)

Hey come here.

(gesturing toward the blond)

What's she drinking?

                          BARTENDER
A martini.

                          LOWELL
Send one over on me.

The bartender pours the drink and takes it
over. Lowell straightens his jacket and runs
his hand through his hair. When she looks over
to see who sent the drink, Lowell smiles and
raises his glass. Smoothing his hair again
Lowell gets off his barstool and steadies
himself before going over meet her, obviously
trying to hide the fact that he's drunk.

                          LOWELL
Is this seat taken?

                    WOMAN
Be my guest.

                    LOWELL
I was sitting over there
trying to think of some
great opening line to say,
but the only thing that
kept running through my
head was, "What's your
sign?"

          (smiling)

So here goes. What's your
sign?

                    WOMAN
               (laughing)

Virgo.

                    LOWELL
               (laughing)

Great. I'm a Cancer. I
think that means it's
written in the stars for
us. Our karma is good or
something like that… My
name's Lowell.

                    WOMAN
             (still smiling)

I'm Susan

                    LOWELL
          (trying to be charming)

Well Susan, were you
suitably impressed by that
dazzling opening line.

                    SUSAN
             (playing along)

I melted when you asked
what my sign was.

Susan's eyes are shining and she is obviously attracted to Lowell.

> LOWELL
> I was going to ask you why you were sitting over here all by yourself, but why should I question my good fortune.

Susan blushes, and there's an awkward pause.

> SUSAN
> Well, Lowell what do you do when you're not out sweeping innocent women off of their feet.

> LOWELL
> I'm an attorney by day, but whenever I'm not being an attorney I can assure you I specialize in being romantic and charming… And what do you do when you're not enticing mortal men with your devastating beauty.

> SUSAN
> I'm an interior designer.

> LOWELL
> Really! It just so happens that my apartment is sorely in need of a new look.

> SUSAN
> (mock surprise)

> Well how long has it needed this new look?

> LOWELL
> Since about twenty minutes ago. But it really is an emergency. Could you

possibly come over and take
a look at it.

There's a pause while Susan considers Lowell's
invitation.

                    LOWELL
            (trying to be convincing)
        It really is urgent. I
        think we should get over
        there right away.

                    SUSAN
                (relenting)
        Since it's an emergency.

CUT TO:

INT. LOWELL'S BEDROOM-SAME NIGHT

Slow pan of Lowell's bedroom. It's a typical
yuppie bachelor's bedroom. Very hi-tech and all
in black. Clothes are strewn all over the
place. Susan and Lowell are lying on the bed
and have obviously just finished having sex.
Susan looks around the room and then rolls on
to Lowell's chest.

                    SUSAN
                (playfully)
        This is my best work yet.

Lowell is sober now, and his face looks like
his mind is somewhere else.

                    LOWELL
                (distracted)
        What?

                    SUSAN
                (giggling)
        Your place looks great now.
        I got here just in time.

Your were right it was an
emergency.

Susan kisses Lowell and he barely responds, but
she doesn't notice.

                    SUSAN
                (more serious)

When I get to work on this
place we can go pick out
some colors that we both
like We need to brighten
things up a bit. Maybe we
can even get some plants.

                    LOWELL
                (uninterested)

Uh… Yeah sure.

Susan still doesn't notice Lowell's apathy.

                    SUSAN
                (self involved)

When we have lunch on
Monday we can decide on the
look we want… I wish I
could stay here all day
tomorrow, but I promised my
mother we'd go shopping and
have dinner. She'll want to
hear all about you, I'm
sure…

                (pause)

Oh, I know a great little
Italian place where we can
have dinner next week…

While Susan is talking we see a close up of
Lowell with a distracted, faraway look on his
face obviously not paying attention to Susan.
His mind is on Sharon.

CUT TO:

EXT. DANCE HALL

Kurt pull the car in front of a forties style
ballroom dance hall.

>   SHARON
>   What's this? Is this where
>   we're going?

CUT TO:

INT. DANCE HALL-SATURDAY NIGHT

Sharon and Kurt are seated at a table on the
edge of the dance floor. A big band is playing
old standards (i.e. Isn't It Romantic) Kurt is
ordering champagne. Sharon is obviously
impressed.

>   KURT
>   Give me a bottle of your
>   best champagne.

>   WAITER
>   Dom Perignon?

>   KURT
>   That will be fine.

>   SHARON
>   (apprehensive)

>   Kurt I'm not dressed for
>   this. Why didn't you tell
>   me? I don't really know how
>   to dance like that. What if
>   I trip and fall?

>   KURT
>   (reassuring)

>   Don't worry about a thing.
>   You look beautiful. Just
>   relax, I'll lead.

He takes her hand and leads her on to the dance
floor. They dance to something very romantic.

They dance well together, but nothing fancy.
The other patrons, who are all elderly couples
look on and smile. Sharon's face is glowing.

CUT TO:

EXT. RESTRUARANT-NIGHT

Kurt's Porsche pulls up to a very expensive
looking restaurant with valet parking.

INT. RESTAURANT

Kurt and Sharon are sitting in a very romantic
booth with champagne and caviar on the table.
Kurt is holding one of Sharon's hands in both
of his hands.

> SHARON
> No one's ever taken me
> dancing like that before. I
> felt like I was in one of
> those old movies… It was so
> romantic.

> KURT
> (smiling)
>
> Ginger Rogers would have
> been proud.

> SHARON
> (also smiling)
>
> I don't think I could
> compare with her.
>
> (pause)
>
> It was really special
> though.

> KURT
> (seriously)
>
> You're a special woman. I
> know we haven't known each
> other very long but I feel
> like this is the beginning

of something really good
between us.

                    SHARON
                (emotionally)

Oh, Kurt I feel the same
way.

                    KURT
                (seems relieved)

Really? I was hoping this
wasn't just another date
for you, because it's more
than that for me.

Kurt, who is holding one of Sharon's hands,
kisses her hand and looks deeply into her eyes.

                    KURT
                (seriously)

        I...

He acts as if he wants to say something, and
then he stops himself. Sharon is still looking
at him dreamy eyed. Kurt then breaks the
awkward pause.

                    KURT
                (chuckling)

        I'm going to wind up
        getting emotional here in a
        minute.

                    SHARON
                (seriously)

        Let's go home.

CUT TO:

INT. SHARON'S BEDROOM-NIGHT

Sharon and Kurt have obviously finished making
love. Sharon is sound asleep and Kurt is lying
back smoking a cigarette. After he finishes his

cigarette, Kurt begins to get dressed. Once he's fully dressed he leaves the room and returns with a rose. Kurt stops for a moment to look at Sharon, and put the rose on the pillow next to her. He lights another cigarette and leaves.

CUT TO:

INT. SHARON'S BEDROOM-SUNDAY MORNING

Sharon awakes with a smile on her face. She reaches across the bed and discovers that Kurt isn't there. She turns to look, and sees the rose.

> SHARON
> Kurt..? Kurt..?
>
> (VO to Patti)
>
> I thought he would be right back.

Sharon eats breakfast slowly. She remembers that she never called her mother back. She starts to call her but first she checks her answering machine.

> LOWELL
> (angry and yelling)
>
> God damit Sharon, what the hell is going on? I want to know where I stand! I don't need this shit! Who the fuck do you think you are?

The telephone slams down on the other end. Sharon is jolted by the message, and looks at the answering machine. The machine beeps for the next message.

> LOWELL
> (calmer and somber)
>
> Sharon it's me again… I'm sorry I got so upset, but…

Just give me a call so we
can talk.

The telephone rings as the message ends. Sharon
grabs the phone on the first ring.

>   SHARON
>   (excited)

Kurt!?

>   MOTHER
>   (laughing)

Sorry to disappoint you
dear but it's not Kurt.

>   SHARON
>   (disappointed)

Oh hi mom.

>   MOTHER
>   (curious)

So who's Kurt?

>   SHARON
>   (confused and scattered)

You know I'm not really
sure. I met Kurt Friday
afternoon in the mall. He's
really cute and charming,
and sometimes when I'm with
him… I just feel like I
don't want to live with out
him, and I'm not sure why.
The thing is I hardly know
him. It's really strange. I
mean we talk about
everything. He listens to
me and he seems supportive
of the things I want to do.
But, he doesn't talk about
himself much. He's not
really shy… Sometimes he
really frustrates me
though. I don't know…

MOTHER
Hmm... Maybe you should try
to get him to talk about
himself more. But first you
should figure out how you
feel. Sometimes you have to
look deep inside to try and
sort out you feelings. But
then you know what they
say, women care about me
and men care about
themselves... Except maybe
for Lowell.

              (pause)

Oh, sorry Sharon I have to
go, your father's calling
me.

        (away from the phone)

Ok Frank I'm coming.

          (back to Sharon)

Talk to you later dear. I'm
sure everything will work
out.

               SHARON
Bye mom.

Seconds after Sharon puts the phone down it
rings again.

               SHARON
              (flatly)

Hello.

          FEMALE VOICE
Hi. Is Kurt there?

               SHARON
              (jolted)

What? Who is this? What
the...

Before Sharon can finish asking the question.

                        FEMALE VOICE
                  Oh never mind here he is
                  now.

The line goes dead.

                        SHARON
                        (yelling)

                  Hello! Hello! Is anyone
                  there? Hello?

Sharon sits there for a few seconds looking at
the telephone.

                        SHARON (VO)
                        (to Patti)

                  And then I started to feel
                  sick. Worse than PMS. My
                  mind was racing through the
                  possibilities. It could
                  have been his mother, but
                  she didn't sound old
                  enough. Maybe his sister?
                  Is he married? How many
                  others are there? What
                  about what he said last
                  night?

Sharon begins to cry. She puts her head in her
hands and sobs uncontrollably.

DISSOLVE TO:

EXT. OUTDOOR SIDEWALK-CLOUDY AFTERNOON

Some time has passed and Sharon decides to go
for a walk. She walks the streets aimlessly.

                        SHARON (VO)
                        (to Patti)

                  By this time I'm trying to
                  be very rational and
                  logical. I hardly know this

guy I say to myself. I met
him on Friday and it's only
Sunday. I can't be this
hung up on him. The whole
time in the back of my mind
I know it's all bullshit
and there's no denying the
way I feel.

CUT TO:

INT. LUNCH RESTAURANT

Sharon is back at lunch with Patti. She has
finished telling her story and she's drained.
Patti also looks drained.

>   PATTI
>   So what are you going to do
>   now?

>   SHARON
>   (gives Patti a long look)
>
>   I don't know. What do you
>   think I should do?

>   PATTI
>   (anxiously)
>
>   Well, we all know there are
>   only two kinds of men in
>   this world, those who care
>   about themselves first and
>   everyone else second, and
>   those who only care about
>   themselves. So what you
>   need to do is figure out
>   which kind Kurt is. He
>   sounds to me like he only
>   cares about himself, but
>   you'll have to decide that
>   for yourself.

>   SHARON
>   I know. I know… I just hope
>   he's not married. I hate

the thought of being the
other woman.

                    PATTI
What difference would that
make?

                    SHARON
               (surprised)

Patti!

                    PATTI
Really Sharon, it's not so
bad.
               (whispers)
I've been one myself.

                    SHARON
               (disbelief)

When?

                    PATTI
Remember Robert.

                    SHARON
               (pause)

Oh that's right.

                    PATTI
I felt the same way about
him as you do about Kurt.
               (wistfully)
I was on a cloud. I was
really in love with him.

                    SHARON
So what happened with him,
anyway?

                    PATTI
He broke my heart. But see,
that's the point. I knew

the pain was coming
eventually.

                    SHARON
I think the pain comes no
matter what you do.

                    PATTI
You're absolutely right.
It's always just a matter
of time until something
happens in a relationship
and you find yourself
waiting for some guy to
call. And then crying your
eyes out when you don't
hear from him.

                    SHARON
Is it all their fault? I
keep thinking maybe I'm
doing something wrong. I
mean, when I fall in love I
can't hold anything back. I
do everything I can to make
it work. And when I make
love… it's real.

                    PATTI
Trust me Sharon it's their
fault. It's them. I tried
to be like them for awhile.
I tried sleeping around and
telling guys anything I
wanted without meaning any
of it. It just got to be so
hallow and empty that I
couldn't do it anymore
though. Sometimes I wonder
if men have any feelings at
all.

                    SHARON
They must, they're human
aren't they?

PATTI
It's hard to tell from the
way they act. I can't
believe how they use
people.

SHARON
They're not the enemy
Patti. Besides, there are
some men who are sensitive
to how a woman feels, or at
least they act like they
are.

PATTI
(laughing)

Yeah, but they're all gay,
married or boring.

A waiter comes to Sharon and Patti's table.

WAITER
Is everything to your
satisfaction ladies?

PATTI
(with mock annoyance)

No, why are men such jerks?

SHARON
(laughing)

Patti!

WAITER
(laughing)

I'm innocent, but whatever
he did it couldn't have
been that bad.

PATTI
Typical. They all stick up
for each other. It's like
a brotherhood of thieves.

                    WAITER
               (still playing along)
          I hope this won't affect my
          tip.

                    PATTI
          Get me a waitress.

                    SHARON
          Don't listen to her.
          Everything was just fine.

The waiter leaves the table.

                    PATTI
          Well have you decided what
          you're going to do about
          Kurt?

                    SHARON
          I'm going to find out
          everything I can about
          Kurt. I'm just afraid I
          won't like what I find.

CUT TO:

INT. L.A. MAGAZINE STAFF ROOM-DAY

Sharon is sitting at her desk trying to work,
but se can't seem to concentrate. She starts
working but winds up just staring at her
computer screen. Frustrated, she reaches for
the phone and calls her mother.

CUT TO:

EXT. SHARON'S PARENTS BACKYARD GARDEN

Sharon's mother is kneeling in a flower bed
working in the garden when she hears the
telephone ring.

INT. SHARON'S PARENTS HOUSE

Sharon's parents home is a comfortable and lived in middle class tract home. Sharon's mother is seen answering the ringing phone.

                    MOTHER
          Hello.

CUT TO:

INT. L.A. MAGAZINE STAFF ROOM

                    SHARON
                    (flatly)
          Hi mom… What're you doing?

CUT TO:

INT. SHARON'S PARENTS HOUSE

                    MOTHER
          Oh, I was just in the
          garden puttering around. My
          flower bed is really going
          to look great in a couple
          of months.

CUT TO:

INT. L.A. MAGAZINE STAFF ROOM

                    SHARON
          That's great mom…

CUT TO:

INT. SHARON'S PARENTS HOUSE

                    MOTHER
                    (pause)
          Want to talk about it dear?

CUT TO:

INT. L.A. MAGAZINE STAFF ROOM

                          SHARON
                       (distressed)
          I guess it's obvious isn't
          it?

CUT TO:

INT. SHARON'S PARENTS HOUSE

                          MOTHER
          I'm your mother. I'm
          supposed to know when
          something's bothering you.

CUT TO:

INT. L.A. MAGAZINE STAFF ROOM

                          SHARON
          I'm just so confused... When
          you were my age you already
          had a husband and a family.
          You had a real life with
          real responsibility. I want
          all of that too. The house,
          the husband, the family,
          everything... I just want to
          make sure I've got the
          right man. Is that such a
          crime? I'm beginning to
          wonder if he even exists,
          someone who can be a good
          husband and father and
          still be exciting and
          romantic.

CUT TO:

INT. SHARON'S PARENTS HOUSE

                          MOTHER
          I know it must be difficult
          dear. You're just going to
          have to be patient. You
          know that I want you to get
          married more than anyone,

but I'd rather have you
wait and be happy, than
have you get into a
relationship that doesn't
work.

CUT TO:

INT. L.A. MAGAZINE STAFF ROOM

               SHARON
 I know… I've just been
waiting so long. Sometimes
I get discouraged. And
let's face it, I'm not
getting any younger. I'm
almost in that age group
that has a better chance of
getting killed by a
terrorist than of getting
married. I'm really going
to have to give a lot of
thought to starting a
family at my age.

CUT TO:

INT. SHARON'S PARENTS HOUSE

               MOTHER
Sharon you know that in
this day and age women of
all ages have children with
no trouble at all. Now stop
being so gloom. There are
always brighter days ahead.

CUT TO:

EXT. GLASS TWOER OFFICE BUILDING-DAY

CUT TO:

INT. KURT'S OFFICE

Kurt's office is very hi-tech. He has a large
glass desk with a modern high back leather
chair. All of the items in his office are
either black or white. Kurt is leaning back in
his chair smoking and talking on the phone.

                    KURT
                (sweetly)

I was thinking about you
the whole weekend. I even
had a dram about you. And
it was one of those kinds
of dreams… You were
incredible.

                (pause)

Yes I'm serious.

                (pause)

Kim if I hadn't been
working all weekend we'd
both be a wreck by now.

Kurt's secretary buzzes him on the intercom.

                    KURT
Hold on for a second Kim

                (agitated)

Yes Carol.

                    CAROL
Dennis Kasten on line two.

                    KURT
                (angrily)

Tell him to fuck off!

                    CAROL
This is the third time he's
called and he said he's
going to keep calling until
you talk to him.

Kurt begins to pace back and forth in front of
his desk.

                    KURT
            Ok. Give me a minute.

             (to Kim on the other line)

            Kim, duty calls. I've got
            to take care of some
            business. How about dinner
            tomorrow?

                  (pause)

            Great, I'll talk to you later.

            (angrily on the line with Kasten)

            Kasten, the deal's off!

                  (pause)

            I don't care how much money
            you'll lose. You should've
            thought about that before
            you started picking up
            those little girls. I told
            you to give that shit up,
            but you wouldn't listen.

                  (pause)

            Look Dennis you're too hot
            right now. When this thing
            blows over we'll talk.
            Until then, stop calling
            me!

Kurt slams the phone down and light another
cigarette. He then buzzes his secretary.

                    KURT
            Carol, call the florist and
            have them send a dozen
            roses to Kim. You know the
            address.

Kurt once again reclines in his chair and
clasps his hands behind his head smiling to
himself.

CUT TO:

INT. L.A. MAGAZINE STAFF ROOM

Sharon begins to investigate Kurt using her skills as a reporter. First, she is on the phone.

> SHARON
> Information? Yes, I'd like the number for a Kurt Warner.
>
> (pause)
>
> Los Angeles. Do you have an address also? Thanks.

Sharon scribbles the information on a piece of paper and hangs up. She then turns to her computer. First she accesses DMV's computer and enters Kurt's name, address, and telephone number. Kurt's driving record comes up on the computer screen along with his driver's license number. She then accesses TRW's computer and enters Kurt's name address and drivers license number. Kurt's complete credit history comes up on the screen, including his personal and business financial information. His marital status is also there. He's divorced. Sharon sits back in her chair and stares at the screen.

CUT TO:

INT. MODELING STUDIO

Sharon goes to see Patti at one of her modelling assignments. Patti is modelling a skimpy bathing suit for a beer advertisement. It's a typical photo studio with cameras, lights, and dozens of people going about their respective jobs. Once she's finished Patti comes over to Sharon.

                    SHARON
I don't know how you can do
this for a living. It's so
degrading.

                    PATTI
Hey it pays the bills, and
besides it's a great
confidence builder. Knowing
that millions of men want
me somehow helps my ego.

          (pause)

So did you find out
anything about Kurt?

                    SHARON
I found something out
alright. He's divorced.

                    PATTI
Did he lie and say he'd
never been married?

                    SHARON
No. He just kind of avoided
giving me a straight answer
when I asked him about it.

                    PATTI
That's as bad as lying. The
bastard.

                    SHARON
I also found out he's worth
a lot more money than I
thought. He's really
loaded.

                    PATTI
Maybe he's not such a
bastard after all. Anyway,
why do you put yourself
through this kind of thing
Sharon? You don't need
this, you've got Lowell.

SHARON

I know.

(pause)

I want to have children
soon, and I know my
biological time clock is
ticking, but I still want
the right man.

PATTI

Lowell's not the right man?

SHARON

He could be, but what if
there's someone else who's
more right?

(pause)

Sure, I'll admit that I
want the white picket
fence, the Volvo and all
that. I just don't want to
be one of those bored
housewives who doesn't have
a real man for a husband.

PATTI

Oh. You mean prince
charming, the man who can
do it all. Let me tell you
Sharon, he doesn't exist.
There is no superman.

SHARON

Well I can still try to get
as close as I can.

PATTI
(sceptical)

So is Kurt this prince
charming?

SHARON

He could be… I still have
some checking to do.

Patti shakes her head and gives Sharon a look of pity.

CUT TO:

EXT. STREET SCENE-NIGHT

Sharon is in her car parked across the street from Kurt's apartment building.

CUT TO:

INT. SHARON'S CAR

Sharon is sitting in her car drinking coffee, staring at the building. She sees Kurt come out of his building arm in arm with a woman. They go into the parking garage and seconds later Kurt's Porsche comes out. Sharon spills her coffee rushing to start the car so she can follow them.

CUT TO:

EXT. RESTAURANT

Kurt's Porsche pulls in the valet parking at the same restaurant he took Sharon on their first date. Sharon pulls up across the street.

CUT TO:

INT. SHARON'S CAR

Sharon sees them get out of the car. Kurt kisses the woman before they go in to the restaurant. Sharon buries her face in her hands.

CUT TO:

EXT. APARTMENT BUILDING-LATER THAT NIGHT

Kurt pulls up in front of another apartment building and Sharon parks across the street. Kurt and the woman go into the building and

Sharon stares after them. As Sharon is driving away tears are streaming down her face.

CUT TO:

EXT. OFFICE BUILDING-DAY

A crowded street with people going in and out of a high rise office building.

CUT TO:

INT. LOBBY OF BUILDING

As Patti is getting in one elevator she sees Lowell getting out of another elevator.

                    PATTI
                  (waving)

          Lowell! Lowell!

Lowell doesn't see her at first.

                    LOWELL
          (depressed and dragging)

          Oh. Hi Patti. What are you
          doing here?

                    PATTI
          My agent is in this
          building. How about you?

                    LOWELL
          I had to take a deposition
          for a client on the
          fourteenth floor.

                    PATTI
          I hate to tell you this
          Lowell, but you look awful.

                    LOWELL
          I know. Everyone keeps
          asking me what's wrong.

PATTI
Well what is wrong? I know
you and Sharon are having
problems, but you don't
have to fall to pieces.

LOWELL
(raising his voice)

Having problems!? I caught
her in her apartment with
some guy who was half
naked!

PATTI
(looking around embarrassed)

Calm down Lowell.

LOWELL
I know, I know. I really
need to get a grip on
myself… Do you have a few
minutes. I need to talk to
someone. Do you want to get
some coffee or something?

PATTI
Sure. My agent doesn't want
to see me anyway. All I
ever do is complain.

LOWELL
Thanks. We can go down to
Café Capaccino.

CUT TO:

INT. COFFEE SHOP

Trendy coffee shop that has all the latest
types of coffee and tea. Patti and Lowell are
sitting at a table by the window.

LOWELL
I don't know what happened.
I thought Sharon and I had

something good going. Why
didn't she say something?

                    PATTI
Just give her some time
Lowell.

                    LOWELL
          (raising his voice again)
Time! How much time does
she need? We've been
together for over a year.

                    PATTI
It's probably just a stage
in your relationship. Once
you get past this point
you'll be closer than ever.

                    LOWELL
You think so? Has she said
anything to you?

                    PATTI
                 (pause)
She's just confused right
now. If you and Sharon were
meant to be things will
work out between the two of
you. Trust me.

                    LOWELL
             (sarcastically)
Yeah, great. Now it's in
the hands fate… It's bad
enough being angry at
Sharon, now I have to deal
with my own conscience.

                    PATTI
What do you mean?

                    LOWELL
Well… I don't know if I
should tell you this is or

not… Oh what the hell. I
guess it doesn't really
matter now. After I caught
Sharon with that other guy,
I went out and got drunk…

                    PATTI
That's not so bad.

                    LOWELL
That's not all… I sort of
had a one night stand.

                    PATTI
Lowell, how do you sort of
have a one night stand?

                    LOWELL
See that's why I feel like
such a shit. For me it was
a one night stand, for her
it was something more.

                    PATTI
What happened, what'd you
do?

                    LOWELL
Well I was sitting in this
bar doing some pretty heavy
drinking. I was depressed
and angry… I felt like
somebody had ripped me
apart. Anyway I'm drinking,
and the more I drink, the
more I think I've got to do
something about this. After
I rule out killing all
three of us, I happen to
look around the bar.
Sitting in a booth all by
herself is a beautiful
blond. She was wearing
white and I swear she was
glowing. I'm talking about
a real angel here. In my

anguish I think, 'here's my
chance to strike back at
Sharon and all of womanhood
for what they've done to
me. So I go over and lay it
on so thick that she can't
resist. The next thing you
know we're back at my place
and she's spending the
night…

                    (pause)

The worst part is that I'm
doing to her the same thing
that Sharon's doing to me.
She thinks this is the
beginning of a great
relationship for her.
Sooner or later I'm going
to have to cut her heart in
pieces just like Sharon did
mine…

Patti pauses for a few moments to think.

                    PATTI
Maybe it's not as bad as
you think. It was only one
night. It could have been a
one nighter for her too.

                    LOWELL
Believe me it's that bad. I
made plans and commitments
and everything. She bought
the whole story. We're
supposed to have dinner
tomorrow… I've never been
the type to do this kind of
thing. And I hate the fact
that some men will say
anything to a woman just to
get what they want. I guess
I'm one of them now.

PATTI
You've got to tell her the
truth Lowell! Whatever you
do, cut it off now. She
probably wants you to meet
her parents by now. Why
haven't you told her yet?

LOWELL
I didn't know what to say.
And, I didn't want to hurt
her. I know how it feels.
Besides, I've been trying
to figure out what to do
about Sharon.

PATTI
Before you even think about
Sharon you've got to level
with this girl! The longer
you wait the worse it will
be for both of you If you
want to get back together
with Sharon you're going to
have to pull yourself
together first.

LOWELL
You're right. I've got to
set thing straight and put
my life back in some kind
of order.

CUT TO:

EXT. OLDER OFFICE BUILDING-AFTERNOON

CUT TO:

INT. LOWELL'S OFFICE

Lowell's office is very traditional. It has a
large wooden desk and a dark green leather
sofa. Lowell is at his desk working. He stops
what he's doing and looks as if he's trying to
make up his mind about something. He reaches

for the phone even though he doesn't seem to
want to.

>   LOWELL
>   Hi Susan. It's Lowell. I…
>
>   (pause)
>
> Yes the dinner last night
> was great. Listen Susan, we
> have to talk.
>
>   (pause)
>
> No don't come over. I want
> to do this over the phone
> because I don't think I
> could face you… Look… Susan
> I don't think we should see
> each other anymore.
>
>   (pause)
>
> Because we don't feel the
> same way about each other…
> I'm not in love with you.
>
>   (pause)
>
> Susan are you there? Oh,
> don't start crying, this is
> tough enough as it is.
>
>   (pause)
>
> Well… Yes there is someone
> else, but I knew her long
> before I met you. I know it
> doesn't help, but I'm
> sorry. I never meant for
> this to happen.

Screaming can be heard from the other end of
the phone as Lowell holds the receiver away
from his ear. When Susan has obviously slammed
the phone down, Lowell looks at the receiver
and shakes his head.

>   LOWELL
>   (angrily to himself)
>
> Shit!

The phone rings just after Lowell had put it
down.

> LOWELL
> (flatly)

Hello.

> (pause)

Dennis would you stop
calling me? I told you I'm
doing everything I can. I
never should have taken
your case in the first
place. I'll let you know if
there are any new
developments, now stop
calling me!

Lowell slams the phone down and begins to rub
his face with his hands. He then reaches for
the intercom.

> LOWELL

Mrs. Simpson would you try
Sharon again for me?

After a few moments the intercom buzzes.

> MRS. SIMPSON

I'm still getting her
machine.

> LOWELL
> (depressed)

Thanks.

Lowell remains sitting at his desk dejected and
drained.

CUT TO:

INT. SHARON'S APARTMENT

The doorbell rings. Sharon answers the door
still sobbing. Patti rushes into the apartment.

PATTI
(concerned)

My God Sharon. I thought
you were going to kill
yourself the way you
sounded on the phone.

SHARON
(whimpering)

Thanks for coming over
Patti.

(pause)

I'm not crazy. My heart is
just broken again… Why does
it have to hurt so much?

Patti puts her arm around Sharon as she starts
to sob again.

PATTI
(soothing)

I know, I know. It's never
the end of the world, it
just feels that way.

Patti rocks Sharon as she would a crying child
until she calms down.

PATTI
You let yourself fall in
love too easily. That's why
you always get hurt.

SHARON
(still snivelling)

I know, but I can't help
it. It always feels so
right. When I get involved
I really believe in a
relationship. I should have
known better.

PATTI

You've got to learn to take
it slow and get control of
your emotions.

Sharon stops to contemplate this point.

SHARON
(emotional)

It just doesn't work like
that for me. I've got to
follow my heart wherever it
leads me. I'm always afraid
that if I cut off my
feelings I'll wind up being
alone and lonely for the
rest of my life.

PATTI

Sometimes I feel that way
too...

(pause)

So we keep getting hurt to
avoid being alone. But
don't we all wind up being
alone in the end anyway?

SHARON
(with resolve)

Maybe so, but you've got to
keep on trying. That's what
it's all about isn't it?

PATTI

I don't know... I guess so...

(smiling weakly)

This is getting a little
too deep for me.

(pause)

So what are you going to do
about Kurt?

Sharon quickly remembers the source of her
anguish, and puts her head in her hand.

> SHARON
> (distraught)

I don't know.

> PATTI
> (firmly)

Well you can't just let him
get away with this. Go over
there and confront him
about it.

> SHARON
> (meekly)

You really think I should?

> PATTI
> Absolutely! Have it out
> with him.

CUT TO:

EXT. UPSCALE SHOPPING MALL

CUT TO:

INT. EXPENSIVE DEPARTMENT STORE

Patti and Sharon are in the cosmetics section
of the store. It's very bright and colourful,
with mirrors everywhere. They are looking over
a wide selection of cosmetics products in every
color imaginable.

> PATTI
> Come on Sharon admit it,
> shopping makes you feel
> better no matter what your
> problem is. It really is
> theraputic.

                    SHARON
          It does take your mind of
          things for awhile…

                    PATTI
               (proud of herself)

          Shopping can cure almost
          anything. If I've got a
          problem or something is on
          my mind, I just head for
          the nearest mall. But, if
          it's something too serious
          for shopping, I'll get a
          complete makeover. Massage,
          facial, hair, nails, the
          works… It's almost as good
          as sex. If a full body
          makeover can't cure you
          then you're beyond help.

Sharon and Patti continue to pore over the
multitudes of cosmetic products.

                    PATTI
          After this we can go over
          to the jewelry department.
          Jewelry is another of
          life's great pick me ups.
                    (pause)
          Oh shit!

                    SHARON
          What's wrong?

                    PATTI
          Ex-boyfriend at twelve
          o'clock. I hate when this
          happens. Maybe he won't see
          me.

                    SHARON
          Where? Which one is he?

Patti, trying to be inconspicuous, points out a
very attractive man in his early thirties.

                    PATTI
          See the really great
          looking guy over the left…
          That's Tim. Thank god he's
          alone. I couldn't face
          seeing my replacement… Oh
          great, I've been spotted.

TIM heads directly toward Sharon and Patti.

                    TIM
                 (smiling)

          Hi Patti. Long time no see.

                    PATTI
                 (sweetly)

          Tim! It has been awhile.
          How are you?

                    TIM
          Great, I've been getting a
          lot of really good
          assignments lately and my
          agent is working on getting
          me a cover.

                    PATTI
          That's wonderful…

Sharon nudges Patti to get an introduction.

                    PATTI
          Oh Tim this is my friend
          Sharon. Sharon this is Tim.
          He's a model too.

                    SHARON
          Hi Tim.

                    TIM
          Hello.

                    PATTI
                (impatiently)

Well Tim, I'm glad things
are going so well for you.

                    TIM

Yeah. It was really great
to see you Patti. You
really look… fantastic.
Give me a call sometime

                    PATTI
                (anxious)

Ok. Well we've got some
heavy shopping to do…

                    TIM
                (laughs)

Ok. I'll see you later
Patti. It was nice meeting
you Sharon.

                    SHARON

It was nice meeting you
too.

                    PATTI

Bye Tim.

Tim walks away and Patti and Sharon look after
him for a few seconds, and then they resume
their shopping.

                    SHARON

Well…?

                    PATTI

Well what?

                    SHARON

Are you going to tell me
why you broke up with Mr.
Wonderful, or do I have to
drag it out of you?

                    PATTI
It's very simple, the word
commitment is not in his
vocabulary.

          (wistfully)

God I was in love with him…
He does look fabulous
doesn't   he… My heart hurts
a little just seeing him
again.

Patti stops and seems to be remembering her
experiences with Tim.

                    PATTI
          (becoming angry)

The real reason we broke up
was that he couldn't decide
who he loved more, me or
himself. You know what he
told me once? He said he
never has to ask women for
dates because they ask him
first. All he has to do is
sit back and wait. The
worst part is that it's
true. I asked him out
before he asked me.

          (pause)

Let's just say he had
trouble saying no when I
wasn't around.

                    SHARON
          (disbelief)

How could he do something
like that?

                    PATTI
          (shrugs)

It's a buyers market… There
are more of us than there

are of them so they know
they can get away with it.

                SHARON
            (pause)

What ever happened to
feminism?

                PATTI
You can't snuggle up to
feminism on a cold winter
night, and feminist men are
on the decline.

            (pause)

What's really terrible is
that the older you get the
worse off you are. Men can
stay single forever with no
problem, but our market
value only lasts so long.

                SHARON
            (sarcastically)

Well that's just great! I
wonder when my stock's
going to bottom out… We're
not commodities that can be
bought and sold Patti.

                PATTI
I'm just telling you how
men think. I wish things
were different, but what
can you do? If I could
change the way things work
believe me I would.

                SHARON
            (resigned)

I know… It's just so
depressing.

                    PATTI
          Come on, let's get over to
          jewelry before I start to
          get really depressed.

Sharon and Patti head over to the jewelry
department with their previous conversation
obviously still on their minds

CUT TO:

EXT. TRENDY LOOKING HEALTH CLUB

CUT TO:

INT. HEALTH CLUB

The health spa is very bright with large
mirrors everywhere, and all the latest exercise
equipment. Kurt and PHIL, an attractive man in
his early thirties, have just finished playing
racquetball, and are heading over to the juice
bar.

                    KURT
          You should have been there
          Phil, it was a thing of
          beauty. Kasten was on the
          phone begging me to keep a
          deal alive, and I shot him
          down. This thing's worth a
          bundle to him. Next time
          he'll probably be on his
          hands and knees outside my
          office.

                    PHIL
          What kind of deal is it?

                    KURT
          Land development. It's a
          three million dollar deal,
          but the potential is
          unlimited. I'll probably
          let him in on it after that
          hooker mess dies down. I

told him he'd get caught.
It's his own fault. If he
had any guts he wouldn't
need to pay for it.

                    PHIL
What do mean?

                    KURT
                (laughing)
You married guys… I guess
your wife's got you
brainwashed too.

                    PHIL
                (defensive)
What!? Get the fuck outta
here, I wear the pants in
my house.

                    KURT
Yeah, but does your wife
let you bring other women
home?

                    PHIL
Of course not.

                    KURT
Do you cheat and go out
with other women behind
her back?

                    PHIL
Well… No.

                    KURT
Like I said, you're
brainwashed just like the
rest of the married guys on
this planet. What's really
sad is the single guys who
are already screwed up by
their girlfriends. I met
some poor fool just a few

days ago who was whining
and crying because I fucked
his girlfriend. Now she's
got him right where I've
got her.

                    PHIL
But I don't want any other
women. My wife's enough for
me.

                    KURT
Bullshit Phil! If some
incredible looking chick
wanted to screw your brains
out, no strings attached,
and you could be absolutely
sure that no one would find
out about it you'd do it.
Admit it. Any man in his
right mind would.

                    PHIL
Ok, maybe I would. But that
doesn't happen in real
life. At least not in my
life.

                    KURT
It could if you let it.
Like I said you're
brainwashed like everyone
else… Look Phil, the bottom
line is that men want to
have sex with as many women
as they possibly can, and
any man can screw around as
much as he wants because
women will believe anything
you tell them, as long as
you say it the right way.

                    PHIL
                 (laughing)

Come on Kurt! You can't be
serious.

                    KURT
I'm completely serious!
It's true!

                    PHIL
                 (disbelief)

You can make any woman
believe anything you say?
How?

                    KURT
It's not that hard. Just
say it like you really
believe it, and tell them
what they want to hear.
It's as simple as that. And
you know why they'll buy
it?

                    PHIL
                 (sceptical)

Why?

                    KURT
Because all women still
want some prince charming
to come along and make
their lives perfect. They
want to believe you're Mr.
Right so bad they'll take
all the bullshit you can
hand them and keep coming
back for more.

                    PHIL
No way. Most women are too
smart for that crap.

                    KURT
You'd think so, but this
has nothing to do with
intelligence. It's all that
stuff that mothers still
tell their daughters about
waiting for Mr. Right, and

women needing a man and a
baby to validate their
existence. This kind of
thing goes way back Phil.
If they don't buy into it
they're turning their backs
on everything women have
been programmed for all
through history. This whole
thing is deep. It's fucking
biological.

                    PHIL
You've got it all worked
out don't you? So you don't
ever plan to settle down,
maybe get married again and
have a family?

                    KURT
Sure. I'm just not going to
let it stand in the way of
me having a good time.

                    PHIL
You mean you're already
planning on lying and
cheating on your second
wife too?

                    KURT
You still don't get it do
you? Don't you realize that
monogamous relationships
don't work? It's human
nature. Every marriage is
based on a lie. Either the
man is lying to himself
that he doesn't want any
woman except his wife, or
the woman is lying to
herself that she is the
only woman in her husband's
life. Marriages are all
doomed to failure unless
both the man and the woman

live the same lie. My next
wife's just going to have
to deal with her lie better
than my first wife did.

                    PHIL
What about all those people
who have long happy
marriages? My parents have
been married for over fifty
years.

                    KURT
They figured out how to
deal with the lie. Besides,
in the past women had to
stay with men for economic
reasons. Now, they've got
their own jobs and their
own money. Why do you think
the divorce rate is so
high?

                    PHIL
I don't know Kurt. That's a
pretty cynical outlook.

                    KURT
Like I said you're
brainwashed.

CUT TO:

EXT. LOWELL'S OFFICE BUILDING-NIGHT

CUT TO:

INT. CONFERENCE ROOM

Lowell is working late in the conference room
of his law firm. He has his head in his hands
as MR. CARTER, a senior partner comes into the
room.

                    MR. CARTER
                    (joking)

        Come on Lowell the Franklin
        case can't be that tough.

Lowell looks up. His face is drawn and pale.
His eyes are bloodshot. He looks terrible.

                    MR. CARTER
                    (shocked)

        Goodness Lowell, what's
        wrong!?

Lowell wearily starts to work again.

                    LOWELL
        It's a long story. You
        wouldn't understand.

                    MR. CARTER
        Come on son, let it out. It
        can't be that bad.

                    LOWELL
        Believe me you don't want
        to know.

Mr. Carter takes a moment to think and then
tries another approach.

                    MR. CARTER
        Wait a minute. I know that
        look, only a woman can make
        a man look like that.

Lowell pauses a moment and decides to talk.

                    LOWELL
        I guess it shows. I don't
        know what it is, I just
        can't figure women out.

                    MR. CARTER
                  (knowing sigh)

Lowell my boy, sometimes I
think it's best not to even
try.

                     LOWELL
                   (anxious)

Maybe not… I thought I'd
understand more as I got
older, but it just keeps
getting more and more
confusing. I mean I thought
I'd be settled down and
married by now. Maybe even
have a kid. But I seem to
always wind up being the
nice guy who finishes last…
You know I was watching TV
the other night, I don't
even know what show it was,
but this girl's on the show
who couldn't have been more
than seventeen, and she
said something I can't get
out of my head. She said
that women will always have
the upper hand because
women are liars and men are
idiots.

Mr. Carter bursts out laughing.

                     LOWELL
And I keep thinking about
it, and the more I think
about it the more I know
it's true. Women are liars
and men are idiots and
there's nothing we can do
about it. It's almost as if
we're at their mercy.

                    MR. CARTER
There's probably something
to that Lowell, but you've
got to rise above it. The
whole key to dealing with
women is to realize that
they're insane. You've got
to ride out that wave of
insanity and get to them
when they're rational. And
don't lead with your chin
when you know they're in
that state of insanity or
you'll get knocked on your
butt every time. But most
of all you've got to ignore
them ninety percent of the
time. I guess women are
liars, but men are only
idiots if they believe
them.

CUT TO:

EXT. KURT'S PORSCHE ON THE STREETS-MORNING

CUT TO:

INT. OF KURT'S PORSCHE

Kurt is in his Porsche driving to work. He
checks his watch then reaches down and presses
the memory button on his car speakerphone. He
is immediately connected with his office.

                KURT'S SECRETARY (VO)
            Kurt Warner's office.

                    KURT
            Morning Carol. Do I have
            any messages yet?

                    CAROL
            Yes. Mr. Kasten called
            three times and said it was
            urgent that he speak with

you as soon as possible. He
said the same thing all
three times he called.

                    KURT
                 (laughing)
Next time he calls tell him
I got the messages and I'll
call him back some time
next month. Maybe.

                    CAROL
Ok. Phil called and wanted
to know if you were still
on for squash this
afternoon. He said to give
him a call.

                    KURT
Ok. Anything else?

                    CAROL
One more thing. Kim wants
you to call her. There's no
message, but she said you
knew the number.

                    KURT
            (smiling to himself)
Good. I'll be there in
about an hour.

Kurt disconnects his secretary and dials Phil's
number.

CUT TO:

INT. PHIL'S OFFICE

Phil is working in his office when the
telephone rings. Phil's office is very
traditional. He has a large oak desk with
leather tufted chairs. The entire décor is in
wood and brass.

                         PHIL
          Hello.

CUT TO:

INT. KURT'S PORSCHE

                         KURT
          Phil. Kurt here. What's
          going on?

CUT TO:

INT. PHIL'S OFFICE

                         PHIL
          I just called to see if we
          were still on for squash
          this afternoon.

CUT TO:

INT. KURT'S PORSHCE

                         KURT
          Absolutely. Three o'clock
          sharp.

CUT TO:

INT. PHIL'S OFFICE

                         PHIL
                       (smiling)
          That's right. I reserved a
          court at the club. But are
          you sure you can make it? I
          thought you might have to
          tend to your harem.

CUT TO:

INT. KURT'S PORSCHE

                         KURT
                     (laughing)

          I'll take care of that
          afterward. As a matter of
          fact I think I'll call
          Sharon and tell her she can
          come over tonight.

CUT TO:

INT. PHIL'S OFFICE

                         PHIL
          Which one is Sharon?
          There're so many I can't
          keep track.

CUT TO:

INT. KURT'S PORSCHE

                         KURT
          I didn't tell you about
          her? She's just another one
          of those thirtysomething
          chicks who doesn't know
          what she wants out of life.

CUT TO:

INT. PHIL'S OFFICE

                         PHIL
                     (laughing)

          Oh, and you're going to
          straighten her out?

CUT TO:

INT. KURT'S PORSCHE

                         KURT
                 (mock sincerity)

          Hey, I'm just trying to
          help.

CUT TO:

INT. PHIL'S OFFICE

Another line on Phil's telephone starts to
ring.

> PHIL
> I gotta go my other line's
> ringing. I'll see you at
> three.

CUT TO:

INT. KURT'S PORSCHE

Kurt in his Porsche. Kurt dials Sharon's
number.

> SHARON (VO)
> Sharon Phillips.

> KURT
> Sharon… Kurt. How are you?

A brief silence is heard over the phone. Sharon
is obviously trying to figure out what to say.
Kurt gives his phone a strange look.

> KURT
> Hello… Sharon are you
> there?

We hear Sharon on the other end of the Kurt's
phone. Her voice is cold and steady.

> SHARON
> I didn't think I'd hear
> from you again.

> KURT
> What, just because I
> haven't called in a few
> days? I have been really
> busy at work this week. Let
> me make it up to you. Why

don't you come over for
dinner tonight around
eight?

> SHARON
> (almost yelling)

What!? I wouldn't...

> (pause)

> (her tone softens)

On second thought, I'll be
there. Eight o'clock sharp.

Kurt doesn't notice anything strange about her
behavior.

> KURT
> (smiling to himself)

Great, I'll see you then.

> SHARON
> (slyly)

I'll be looking forward to
it.

After he hangs up the phone, Kurt checks his
hair in the mirror.

> KURT
> (to himself)

I knew she couldn't resist.

CUT TO:

INT. MODELING STUDIO

Sharon has gone to see Patti at her modelling
assignment. The studio is large and very bright
with photographic equipment covering the floor.
Sharon is pacing back and forth as Patti is
having her makeup applied.

                    SHARON
                    (angry)

I can't believe the nerve
of that guy. Can you
believe him?

                    PATTI
                    (calmly)

No, I can't believe it.

                    SHARON

First he uses me and walks
all over me, and now he
wants to wipe his feet.

                    PATTI

Typical.

                    SHARON

He obviously hasn't even
really thought of me as a
person for even one minute.

                    PATTI

Obviously.

                    SHARON

Well you were right Patti.
I think I should go have it
out with him.

                    PATTI

I hate to say I told you
so.

                    SHARON

I'm going over there
tonight and let him have
it. I don't think he
suspects a thing.

                    PATTI

Give him hell Sharon!

CUT TO:

EXT. KURT'S CONDOMINIUM BUILDING-NIGHT

The building is a very expensive looking hi-rise.

CUT TO:

INT. THE HALL OUTSIDE OF KURT'S DOOR

Sharon is in the hall pacing back and forth in front of Kurt's door. She's dressed all in black, and has a very intense look on her face. Every few seconds she mumbles something, as if she were rehearsing a speech.

> SHARON
> (mumbling to herself)
>
> Lying… cheating…
> insensitive…

After more seconds of pacing Sharon stops in front of Kurt's door. She takes a deep breath, gathers her courage and rings the doorbell. After a few seconds Kurt, dressed in a suit and tie, opens the door smiling widely.

> KURT
> I'm so glad you could…
>
> (pause)
>
> make it.

Sharon is standing defiantly at the door with her arms folded across her chest. The smile slowly fades from Kurt's face when he reads Sharon's body language and sees the expression on her face. His expression suddenly becomes cold, hard, and calculating.

> KURT
> I suppose you want to come
> in?

Sharon is slightly taken aback by his suddenly abrupt manner.

                    SHARON
          Well you did invite me… I'd
          just like to talk to you
          for a few minutes if I
          could.

Kurt opens the door wide and motions for her to
come in. Kurt's apartment is very hi-tech.
Everything is electronic, expensive and the
colors are all in black or white. The dining
room table is set for a romantic dinner for
two. Kurt coolly walks over, sits in the middle
of the sofa and lights a cigarette, as Sharon
stands awkwardly in the middle of the living
room.

                    KURT
                 (coldly)

          Well?

                    SHARON
          Well… I just come over to
          tell you that I never want
          to see you again, and… and…
          Well I just can't believe
          how you treated me.

Sharon starts to pace and gain her confidence
as she speaks.

                    SHARON
          You really hurt me. I
          thought I was in love with
          you. And don't act like you
          don't know what I'm talking
          about, because you and I
          both know you're seeing
          other women. It's just
          that… you lead me on. Why
          did you say you loved me?

Sharon's voice begins to tremble and tears well
up in her eyes as she relives the pain she felt
only a few days earlier.

                    SHARON
How can you go around
hurting people like that?
Didn't you think about me
at all? You must not have
any feelings at all.

Tears begin to roll down her cheeks. She wants
to say more be she just can't go on. Her speech
didn't come out the way she planned it, but she
got her point across as beast she could. Kurt
is still silently smoking an emotionless. After
she has obviously finished speaking there is a
long pause as Sharon weeps.

                    KURT
                 (annoyed)

Are you finished?

                 (pause)

You're living in a dream
world babe. You're all
alike. When are you women
going to stop beliving in
this crazy fantasy world
that doesn't exist… How can
you stand there and talk
about how I hurt you or how
I lied to you? Wake up!
There was never anything
between us. That was just
something you wanted to
hear… What did you expect
anyway? We me in the
lingerie section of a
department store! You think
I didn't know what you
wanted to hear the moment I
saw your face? You're
desperate for something
that doesn't exist. Hey!
I've got a news flash for
you, there is no perfect
man. That perfect prince
charming that's supposed to
ride in on the white horse

is just a load of bullshit
that chicks still cling to
because they can't deal
with real life. No one's
going to come along and
solve all your problems.

Kurt pauses to pace around the room and take
another long drag on his cigarette.

                    KURT
          What really pisses me off
          is how hypocritical and
          self-righteous you are. How
          can you stand there and
          accuse me of how I
          mistreated you, well what
          about how you treated Mr.
          Fix-It? What about him?
          What did you tell him? I'll
          tell you exactly what you
          did, you gave him the same
          line of bullshit I gave
          you. So don't come in here
          and give me some sorry
          speech about how much I
          hurt you until you take a
          good long look in the
          mirror... If you really need
          a man to make your life
          complete why don't you go
          back to what's his name,
          maybe he can live in your
          dream world, but don't lay
          your problems off on me!

Kurt sits back down on the sofa and lights
another cigarette. Sharon, who has been
standing in the same place whimpering, bursts
into tears and runs out of the apartment.

CUT TO:

INT. HALLWAY OUTSIDE KURT'S APARTMENT

Sharon is sobbing uncontrollably and stumbles
toward the elevator at the end of the hall.

INT. ELEVATOR

Once she gets in the elevator and the door closes, Sharon screams at the top of her lungs.

> SHARON
> I HATE MEN!!!

CUT TO:

INT. KURT'S APARTMENT

Kurt is still sitting on the sofa smoking when the telephone rings.

> KURT
> Hello... Kasten I thought I told you not to call me anymore... What? Alright, alright.

Kurt reaches for the remote and turns the TV on. The TV shows Kasten and Lowell walking down the steps of the court house.

> TV REPORTER (VO)
> In a surprise decision today all the charges against Dennis Kasten were dismissed. Sources say that lack of evidence was the reason behind the decision. Apparently the whole thing was just a big misunderstanding.

Kurt burst out laughing as he turns the sound down on his TV.

> KURT
> I don't know how you did it Kasten, but you sure pulled it off... Yeah right, you had a good lawyer... Ok. Ok. You're back in the deal you greedy bastard. Who knows,

maybe we can use this thing
to our advantage.

CUT TO:

INT. SHARON'S APARTMENT

As Sharon enters her apartment she stops short
when she sees Lowell standing in the middle of
the living room. They stand there just looking
at each other for a few seconds.

>   LOWELL
>   (emotionally)

Sharon, come over here and
sit down.

They both sit on the sofa as Lowell holds
Sharon's hands and takes a deep breath before
he continues.

>   LOWELL
> I've been trying to figure
> out what to do ever since I
> found you here with that
> other guy. I've been
> racking my brains trying to
> figure out what went wrong,
> or what I did, or
> something… I don't know.
> But I finally realized that
> I don't need to do anything
> except look deep inside my
> heart and understand how I
> really feel about you…
> Sharon, I love you… Maybe I
> wasn't sure before or I was
> afraid of it or something…
> But now I know that I love
> you more than any woman
> I've ever met or even
> dreamed of, and I know deep
> in your heart you love me
> too. If you just listen to
> your heart and forget about
> what you think your life is

suppose to be like, you'll
see that what we've got is
too good to give up on... So
I know I don't have to try
and get you back because
you never really left. Just
listen to your heart,
because I know it's saying
the same thing mine is.
It's saying yes.

Lowell gets down on one knee and reaches in his jacket for a ring.

                    LOWELL
          Sharon, will you marry me?

Sharon immediately begins to cry tears of joy. She embraces Lowell as she seems to be clinging to him for her life.

                    SHARON
                 (breathlessly)
          Yes. Yes. Yes.

FADE TO BLACK

                                        /1993

www.circularmotion.net

For information on new and upcoming publications.

Visit

dash Media NETWORKS
www.dashmedianetworks.com

www.ingramcontent.com/pod-product-compliance
Lightning Source LLC
Chambersburg PA
CBHW051922240626
47153CB00004B/1324